Spreading Joy Daily

Reminding you of the simple JOY of giving.

Momma
Thank you for
always loving me.....
Always!
Mari

Helping you to make a difference where you are, with what you have.

We want to rise above the discouragement of high prices, the obstacle of dead ends and the disappointment of our comfort zone. We want to be the change that is so desperately needed

And

We want you to experience the same!

1

Printed in the United States of America

First Printing, 2012

ISBN 9-781467-997744

Spreading Joy Corporation
PO Box 1771
Denver NC 28037
www.www.spreading-joy.org

Dedicated to my Mom (Mildred Landwehr) and Dad (John Horne Sr.) – the Original Spreading Joy Heroes

Thanks Mom for always seeing the good in others, valuing the positive and showing me with your life how wonderful it is so that I would be inspired to do the same. Thank you for loving me…..unconditionally. I love you more than you may ever know.

Thanks Dad for always giving to others, for not judging when they asked for help and for showing me with your life how wonderful it was so that I would be inspired to do the same. I love you Daddy and miss you horribly.

Spreading Joy Daily book logo and cover was designed by Jordan Tickle. For pricing email him:

jtothetickle289@gmail.com

About Marie Wikle: Seeing through the eyes of compassion and understanding the heart that desires to have an impact, Marie encourages others to see the full potential of the everyday, ordinary resources that is right within their reach.

 Everyone needs to make a difference and with creative thinking and a unique look at the ordinary, she shows people all over the world just how easy it is to make a difference.

Marie is available to speak to your ladies group, child's class room or any social gathering so that you can hear firsthand how to step up, lead the way in innovative thinking and see just how easy the ordinary items of daily living can be used to make a difference.

Contact Marie for more information via email at marie@spreading-joy.org

Here is a look at what Spreading Joy can do for your group:

1. **Empower your children** - Children are so powerful. They have a deep need to feel this as well as to be able to see it. Spreading Joy is about seeing things differently, stepping up and making choices to lead the way in finding the beauty in the ordinary. We encourage your children to make the choice to actively choose joy over choosing to stay in the pits of unhappiness. We encourage them to boldly lead the way with innovative thinking while making a difference for others.

2. **Ladies Groups** - Many ladies walk around with a load of guilt weighing them down. This is unhealthy, unproductive and most of all unnecessary! Stay at home Moms often feel like they are not giving their children the best role models simply because they are not leading some corporate office somewhere. Working Moms sometimes feel like they are cheating their children out of important time and memories

together. We help you to step outside of the "issues" and start focusing on the little things that make life big!

3. Any group - Finding Joy even through sorrow. Happiness and joy is not the same thing at all, as there can be joy through sorrow. We encourage any social group by reminding you that you can make a difference with little to NO resources and enjoy the little things that make life big! Sometimes seeing things from a different set of eyes is all it takes to get the mind going.

4. 30 Days to Spreading Joy - Building JOYful habits that last! Want to be more aware of ways to make a difference? Think that this economy makes it impossible to give back? Feel discouraged because your heart is screaming to give more, do more and your wallet screams louder saying NO WAY? End the struggle and let Spreading Joy show you ways to make a difference without breaking the bank, which will in turn cause your heart to be flooded with great joy!

Any of these things along with a million others can be adjusted to fit the needs of your group. I hope you'll consider allowing us to come and encourage your social group.

January

 January is fresh start, new beginnings and the first step to making a difference daily. This is the time we usually reflect on the past and what we accomplished. Instead of lamenting what you did not accomplish, choose to look forward to new opportunities and resolve to do what you can where you are, with what you have.

As you waltz your way through this month, your mind will start thinking of all the choices you have to make a difference. An entire year of joyfulness awaits you. Let's get going, shall we?

January 1 - Christmas...Again? Sure thing!

Purchase Christmas gifts for "others" through the year. When January 1st rolls around, go ahead and start thinking about what you'd like to donate to some awesome children for Christmas. Start purchasing 2 gifts a month and in December you will be able to JOYfully donate 24 gifts to make a huge difference for someone for Christmas. THAT is pretty awesome if you ask me!

January 2 - Kids, Pizza & NO Dishes!

Joy for your family! Family night! Let the kids choose what to do, what to eat and just go with the flow. It could be movies, games or just chatting around an extra large pizza. No dishes, no cleaning or anytime of work. Prepare to laugh and have fun being together.

January 3 – Uno – YOU Win!

UNO – Give a pack of Uno Cards away to some children in your neighborhood or elsewhere. If you do not know the children, please make sure it is ok with the parent before giving this gift. I use a regular address label and put the spreading joy website on it, so that they will see where the ideas came from. Two acts of joy in one!

January 4 – Mom and Pop shops are Awesome

Support your community by eating out at local food establishments. While I love Outback, I can find one of those nearly everywhere. Look for, eat at and support those smaller, lesser known restaurants in your home town.

January 5 – Spreading the Word...Priceless

Spread the word about Spreading Joy! Email a link to the website and/or forward the newsletter that you receive. Email a link to several of the videos that show you just how easy spreading joy truly is. Spread the WORD!

January 6 – Written Words Are Powerful

Give cards to 5 people today and see just how wonderful your day will turn out. This will take some planning, so get up a little early and get writing. No groaning allowed, unless you stump your toe on the way to the coffee pot. Words have a lasting impression on the heart and today, you will make a wonderful impression.

January 7 – Blankets Give More Than Warmth

Donate your extra blankets to a homeless shelter. You have so many blankets in the closets. You have plenty for the guests that you may or may not have for your various get togethers, so why not pick out half of what you have and take to a homeless shelter? These will go a long way in helping to warm the heart of a kind soul that needs to be wrapped in love as well as warmth.

January 8 – Giving During Lean Times

Give your tithes! Think about it. When is the last time you gave a full 10% of your income? Many people cut out their giving to churches and other Non-Profits when financial times are bad, so this will be a huge help to the church or NPO that you are helping.

January 9 – Do Not Waste Gift Cards

Donate gift cards that you won't use! I can't imagine someone NOT using their Starbucks gift card, but if you happen to receive a gift card that you won't use or can't use, donate it here to Spreading Joy and we will use it as a means of encouraging others.

January 10 – Puzzles With Seniors

Buy a puzzle and work it with someone who can't get out and about. Sometimes the gift of time is the most precious gift ever. Many senior citizens cannot get out and enjoy the company of others, so go to them. Take a seek and find puzzle book, a fruit basket or some delicious snacks to share! Find out if they are diabetic or not. Be sure to plan on spending a few hours laughing, eating and solving puzzles together.

January 11 – The Muffin Man Brings Smiles

Do you know the muffin man (or woman)? BE the muffin man today. Bake several dozens of muffins. Freeze some for breakfast for the family and then take a batch to work and put in the common area. This simple breakfast staple may inspire someone else to do some baking of their own to share with everyone.

January 12 – Welcome To The Neighborhood

Befriend a new neighbor. In this day and age, we don't spend time getting to know those we live near. Take a casserole to them or a basket of coffee cups with flavored coffee creamers. This will be a great ice breaker and get you well on your way to a brand new friendship.

January 13 – Ordinary Becomes Extrordinary

If this 13th day of the year happens to fall on a Friday, celebrate Friday the 13th and do something out of the ordinary! Give a card with a gift certificate in it to a stranger. Write something in the card like, "go for it!" or something encouraging. Don't sign it. Just give it to a random passerby.

January 14 – Hearts Will Sing

Pass on your favorite cd's to a friend as a gift. You've got them saved on your computer as well as a jump drive, so pass them on! Share the gift of song!

January 15 – Cozy, Warm...Special

Sit by a cozy fireplace with your someone special and take some time to remember when you met, your first kiss and other special times that you've shared over the years.

January 16 – Mom Will Rejoice

Conserve Energy and turn out those lights! Moms all over the earth will thank you and so will your electric bill. It amazes me that when people leave a room they forget to reach out, flip a switch and go on. You don't even have to stop, just do it in passing. How many lights are on at your place and the room is empty?

January 17 – Special delivery of Entertainment

Donate gently use DVD's, VHS tapes and video games. Many people just end up tossing these items because there is not enough time to deliver them. Take the time to deliver them as well as maybe find a place that will "give" these items away. Battered Women's shelters are great for this. These ladies and children are starting over and even though the Goodwill stores have cheap prices, many of these ladies cannot even afford those prices. Do good...twice!

January 18 – Remember Missionaries

Support a Missionary. So many wonderful missionaries have given up the comforts of home to go overseas and preach, help and encourage others. Send them a care package or make a financial contribution. No gift is too small. Send a monthly email to them. Need a list? Contact me, I can help with this! I personally know several Missionary Heroes.

January 19 – Emails Encourage Without Effort

Include an encouraging quote at the end of each email. Change them up weekly. Use your signature line feature to do this easily!

January 20 – Waldo Is Hiding From Seniors Too

Where's Waldo? Take these puzzle books to a nursing home! Many residents there will love spending time looking for Waldo and his friends. He has many friends that are hidden in each puzzle too. Have you ever taken the time to look at these? There is so much fun in each scene. Take some time to look with them. They will love the laughter as well as the smiles it produces when you look up at each other, your eyes connect because you finally found him hiding in the balloons.

January 21 – Positively Contagious

Be Positive today. Have you tried this? Sometimes it is so hard! Sometimes you think you've got the negative feelings under wrap and they squirm their way front and center. So many people will benefit from your positive attitude. JOY is contagious... be a carrier!

January 22 – You Work Hard For Your Money

Celebrate your Job! Take a co-worker to lunch and have fun celebrating the fact that you have a wonderful job. Yes, there are things that we don't like about our jobs, but I would dare say there are many more things we love. Laugh, have fun and remember some of the crazy things you've done together.

January 23 – Sweet Treats For Sweet People

Honey - I love those buns! Honey buns that is! Get a box of your favorite honey buns and share.

January 24 – Filling Local Pantries

Donate food to a small local food pantry. Many pantries PAY to get food from Second Harvest food bank and it's at a low rate, but still it can be costly. Make a donation to a small local pantry that is helping people.

January 25 – Your Words Stick to the Heart

Leave a sticky note of encouragement on everyone's computer today. Ok, if you work with 300 people, then you can't leave one for every single person, but you can do it for

some. Don't sign your name to the sticky note, just leave
something encouraging and a smiley face.

January 26 – Movies, More Than an Adventure

Enjoy movie night with the family. This is one of our favorite
ways to treat ourselves. With the expense of tickets and
snacks to go with it, we usually reserve this for when we are
all together. No small feat considering college and other
social activities of teens. Find one that everyone can enjoy,
purchase a large tub of popcorn, sit back, relax and enjoy.

January 27 – Care for College Kids

Send a college kid a care package! Fill it with lots of love and
put in some cold hard cash for eating out and/or laundry.
Make sure you include lots of junk food, snacks and other
yummy things that college kids can not afford to purchase.

January 28 – The Hot Now Light is On

Pick up hot Krispy Kreme donuts for co-workers. Leave a little
earlier in the morning and grab a dozen of the delicious, melt
in your mouth rings of joy. Leave in the common area and
enjoy the laughter and delight of those that are enjoying
themselves.

January 29 – Notes Do Not Go Unnoticed

Give a handwritten note card of encouragement. Think back
to the last time you received a note card that just said "thank
you for being you" and it was not given to you for a special
reason. The card that we send "just because" really
encourages more than we may realize.

January 30 – Simply Delicious

Give away a bag of individual size m&m's. Yummieee! Leave it for a co-worker or on the pillow of your significant other. Leave one on your children's pillow. This sweet surprise will be sure to end in big squishy hugs for you.

January 31 – Little Things Are Huge at Shelters

Package your left over Christmas chocolates and candies and give them to a nearby shelter.

NuggetsofJOY:

> ➢ *Look through the eyes of compassion as you make your way through the day. ~ Marie Wikle*
> ➢ *Take chances, let your voice be heard and make a difference. - Ryan Leite class of 2011*
> ➢ *Create JOY*
> ➢ *We are all fighting a battle. Pain is pain - no matter what kind - it still hurts! I'm glad for friends who help ease it. ~ Marie Wikle*
> ➢ *A happy person is not a person in a certain set of circumstances, but rather a person with a certain set of attitudes. - Hugh Downs*

February

February is the month that many of us celebrate love and being in love. We love to be needed as well as need to be loved so we show all those around us how very special they are. Why not take it up a notch or two and make acts of joy for them an everyday occurrence?   Spreading Joy with someone else is always double the fun.

The element of surprise is so amazing isn't it? Reactions will vary, especially from family members on this journey. Just simply soak up the goodness as you work through each day, looking for ways to make a difference and enjoying the little things that make life big.

February 1 – Comments Encourage Writers

Comment on your favorite Blog. This is a HUGE encouragement for those who take the time to write, encourage and give wisdom where they can! It only takes a moment and plus, you never know what conversation, idea and other friendships will be struck up because of your comment. Don't worry about what you are saying or how others will see it. Speak from the heart and say what is on your mind. Step out of your comfort zone and take the time to make that comment today!

February 2 – Unwrap a Smile

Little Debbie cakes bring such happiness and are so affordable. Give them freely. Put them in your children's lunch box as well as give them to random people. They will be surprised but will smile big when you hand over this delicious treat!

February 3 – Single Moms' Need Computers

Upgrading your computers? Your old one still works? Donate it. There are so many single Moms' who'd benefit from this gift.

February 4 – Support Our Troops

Thank our troops and support them. I love our Military! You'll make a huge difference for them as many feel that because they are often out of sight, they are out of mind. This is completely untrue and we need to do all that we can do to let them know this. You can do this by sending free e-cards online, sending care packages and writing letters. Have fun! Support our Troops!

February 5 – Right That Wrong

Right a wrong. I didn't say all the acts of joy were going to be easy now did I? This is a priceless way of Spreading Joy. In a society where so many people want to blame someone else, you – owning up to your mistake will be something that is unheard of and welcomed. Give it a try and see the difference it makes in your own heart.

February 6 – Magazines Keep Giving

Recycle Magazines by giving them to a women's shelter or even a nursing home. These magazines will get used time and time again. Don't toss them out. Put them to great use!

February 7 – Multitude of Happiness

Spend the day Spreading Joy and happiness everywhere. Literally decide that today, no matter what comes your way, that you'll do as many acts of joy as you can for your family, friends and any strangers that you come in contact with. It could be smiles, special dinners or any number of things in this book. See just how many you can do in one day! I guarantee by the end of the day your heart will be flooded with amazing joy and you'll fall asleep with the biggest smile on your heart, which will be reflected on your face and put a sparkle in your eyes.

February 8 – Partner With Spreading Joy Financially

Make a financial contribution to Spreading Joy. We need monthly partners that will give each month. It doesn't matter the amount, just that you'll make the donation each month. We also need people that will give during special times. Back to school and Christmas Joy are the biggest events we do each year. For our Back to school project our desire is to give back packs filled with the necessary supplies to send kids back to school with their head held high. Christmas Joy is when we give gifts to children that may not get any gifts or just a few. Both of these events are amazing as well as costly. We cannot do this without you. Would you partner with us and help us to make a difference in the hearts of some amazing children? Imagine what 500 people giving $10 each month could do for Spreading Joy.

February 9 – Poetry Lasts A Lifetime

How do I love thee...let me count the ways... I love poetry but I'm not one of these gifted people who can just start writing and great poetry just oozes from their pen. But, I do know how the heart will soar when you hear that you are loved and WHY! It doesn't have to rhyme, but take some time to write out I love….. and then put why for your significant other. Print it off on nice paper and get it laminated. This keepsake will be treasured for a long time to come.

February 10 – Extra Sprinkles Please

Bake & Donate! Give to a shelter or church group! Sprinkle those cookies with love. Top those cupcakes with great joy! Wrap and deliver. You'll sweeten up tummies and put joy in hearts with these sweet treats.

February 11 – Cheesecake, Glorious Cheesecake

Purchase a cheesecake from the store and give it to a neighbor. Put a little note or card on it wishing them a wonderful evening!

February 12 – Treasures of Friendships

Get to know someone that you don't know real well. Really! You may work with this person but because your company is so large, you really don't know them. This may be someone in your church but you are so busy teaching, helping and such that you have not had time to get to really know them. You never know what friendship will form, what you have in common, and just what a blessing it will be to YOU! Lifetime friendships are treasures you can lock inside your heart for an eternity and beyond. Try it! Have fun! Step out of your comfort zone and just say hello.

February 13 – Travel Size Items for Care Kits

Do you travel for business? Don't just leave those toiletries there. Toss them in your suitcase and bring them home. Once you have a bag full of them, take to your local shelter. Better yet, make up a CARE kit for the homeless that you pass. Put these wonderful items in it, along with things that have a long shelf life. Keep a few in your car and when you pass the homeless, you'll have a few kits to hand out of the window to them.

February 14 – Celebrate All Those You Love

Happy Valentine's Day! The day the world celebrates LOVE! Who do you love? It doesn't JUST have to be your special someone. It can be a child, friend, neighbor etc. Take some time to show this love in a special way today. [Whispering] But, don't forget about your special someone either.

February 15 – Half Price is Awesome

Buy some half price Valentine candy and share the wealth. Give some to a local School teacher to use as treats. Give to a local Sunday school teacher for his/her class. You are making a difference and saving some money with the extra discounts.

February 16 – Thoughts of You

Send several emails just to say "thinking of you". Add in a cute little picture and you've just sent several smiles. I love how easy pictures and emails make spreading joy. Nothing like waking to a cute email that says I was thinking of you. Those kind of things start the day off with a smile.

February 17 – Double the Joy

Give a pack/box of note cards to someone. This will enable them to make a difference for others as well as warm their heart. Your act of joy doing double duty! HUGE splashes of joy in your heart for that one!

February 18 – Nieces and Nephews Rock

Make sure your nieces and nephews know that you love them! Regardless of the finances, the "to-do" list and the million other things you have going on, make sure you take the time to tell them how special they really are.

February 19 – Favorites Abound

Make a special meal for your children. Take one week and fix the favorite meal of each of your children. Better yet, why not include your spouse in that? Include their favorite drink and dessert. Sit some of their favorite things out on the table and spend the evening talking about as many of their favorite things that you can come up with. Prepare a list of questions in advance if necessary. For instance, "what is your favorite....." Be sure to only focus on that ONE special person that night.

February 20 – Passing the Kleenex

Sniffles got someone you know down? Put together a neat gift that includes some good ole comfort for them. In a pretty basket or new pot, assemble some delicious chicken soup, box of Kleenex, puzzle book, warm fuzzy socks (if it's a gal), a cd that you've made especially for them, and a magazine or two. Top it off with a cute bow or stuffed animal and they will be feeling better in no time.

February 21 – Handmade Cards and Journals

Are you Crafty? Make some thinking of you or thank you cards and give a pack of 10 of them away. I love giving away these kinds of cards but don't have the time nor the talent to make gorgeous ones. Anyone who would want to make some saying "There's no JOY like Spreading JOY" I'd love that! Besides, who doesn't love getting homemade cards? Homemade Journals are the same in my eyes. I love getting them as well as giving them!

February 22 – Next!!

Offer for someone to go ahead of you in the store or food line. I've been on the receiving end of this joyful act and cannot tell you what an awesome gift it was. I was trying to simply run in, grab 4 huge bags of candy for a school presentation and get out. What I didn't realize was that trying to carry 40 lbs of candy would not go over so well. I managed to get to the cash register and was obviously struggling....with a smile. The gentleman in front of me not only noticed, but allowed me to go ahead of him so that I could place my bags on the counter. I was so thankful and happy that before I realized what I was doing, I had given him a HUGE hug for rescuing me. He laughed and told the party on the other end of the phone that "a strange lady" had accosted him in Sam's. I laughed while apologizing and thanking him all at the same time.

February 23 – Monday, Monday....Can't Trust That Day

Break up the Monday blues by baking a batch of brownies and taking them with you to work. Can you imagine the surprise as well as the delight of your co-workers? I love Mondays that start out "sweet".

February 24 – Dinner for Two Please...but Don't Tell!

Purchase dinner for an elderly couple. You've seen them. They are so cute, walking hand in hand or sitting quietly while their hearts speak volumes to each other. These couples have done so much to inspire many of us, so why not do a little something for them? Call their server over to you and ask for their bill. If you've planned ahead and have one of the several Spreading Joy gift tickets on you, you can leave that, telling them that they are special. Do it...I dare you. It's an amazing feeling. **Today is my brother David's birthday! Happy Birthday, I love you!**

February 25 – While I'm Waiting

Leave used books in the Waiting Room of ER's or Doctor's offices. Many have books and probably will not mind. You could take this one step further and put a label in it saying that

"I'm leaving this to help spread the word about Spreading JOY. Visit www.spreading-joy.org for more ideas and encouragement." Doing this, you'll be spreading joy two ways. Leaving a gift for someone to enjoy and spreading the word about Spreading Joy. How awesome is that?

February 26 – sdrawkcaB is Fun

Have Backwards Night with your family. Seriously! Put on jammies, play Sorry Backwards by starting everyone in "home" and working backwards to "start". Have snacks, then dessert and then dinner. Even wear your jammies backwards and then sit back and enjoy the mile wide smiles and let your heart soak up the laughter.

February 27 – BIG GRINS

Smile at everyone and say hello! OK, I'm NOT even KIDDING, you will make a huge difference here. You never know what a day has held for some people and the kindness of a smile and hello may be all it takes to put their heart and mind in a much better place. Try it for one entire day. If you are not comfortable with that, decide that while you are out and about, you'll smile and say hello to 10 people that you do not know.

February 28 – Companies Love to Match Gifts

Designate your company match to Spreading Joy. Many organizations will match your contributions 100 % up to a certain amount. A call or visit to your HR director and fill out a few things and your match is complete! Check with your company today and see if they match donations made to IRS approved Non-Profits. Doubling your gift for free has never been easier!

February 29 – Stuffed With Goodness

There are always Valentine Teddy Bears left over. At 50% off, you can purchase several of these for gifts for your other's box. They may even be 75% off by now. You'll be able to make a huge difference at Christmas time without breaking the bank early on in the year.

nuggetsofJOY:

> ➢ *Being vulnerable simply means being YOU – Be the one to be honestly, completely, authentically YOU - regardless of how you are feeling. ~ Marie Wikle*
> ➢ *Don't just look for the writing on the wall, listen for the whisper ~ Marie Wikle*
> ➢ *As you attempt to make big differences, remember to appreciate the small differences. And remember that you don't always have to reach the goal you set in order to make a difference.--Win Borden*
> ➢ *For it was not into my ear you whispered, but into my heart. It was not my lips you kissed, but my soul – Judy Garland*
> ➢ *If you want happiness for an hour, take a nap.*
> *If you want happiness for a day, go fishing.*
> *If you want happiness for a year, inherit a fortune.*
> *If you want happiness for a lifetime, help somebody.--Chinese proverb*

March

We enjoy seasonal changes don't we? We understand that the weather will not always be the perfect cool, breezy and sunny day that we love. We enjoy those days and make it through the storms that pop up through the season.

Daily life is just the same. We all have problems and issues that we deal with. Isn't it refreshing to stop thinking about them for just a little while and plan something that will bring a smile to the heart of another? Think about the power you hold. You are perfectly equipped to turn a dreary day for someone into an awesome day – OR you can take a wonderful day and turn it into a magnificent day! May you notice the opportunities to make a difference that are swirling all around you.

March 1 – Box Tops for Education

Turn in those Box Tops for Education that are found on various Pillsbury items. No children in your house you say? I bet you have at least 3 schools in your community that are full of children that will benefit from the few seconds it takes for you to rip off these box tops. Grab yourself a Box Top Jar, start ripping and placing in there. Once a month, drop them off at the school. Simple, effective and full of joy!

March 2 – Lunch is on Me

Take a co-worker out to lunch! Surprise!!! Go to the next department or next row of cubicles and invite someone to go to lunch. They will assume its Dutch treat, but when you get there, surprise them and pick up their tab! If you do this on a Friday or Monday it will be even better! And, if it happens to be a very special birthday, that is even better! It's my sister's birthday! **Happy Birthday Angie**... Lunch is definitely ON me! I love you.

March 3 – Just Because is the Best

Leave your spouse a note just because. Do not attach any assumptions to it. Meaning, don't expect them to reply, acknowledge or anything. Just leave the note saying you love them.

March 4 – Warm Feet, Warmer Hearts

Socks for the Homeless – Donate some packs of socks to your local homeless shelter. We take this for granted so very often. We grab our warm socks, fuzzy socks and even cute toe socks while many of our homeless do not get to enjoy this luxury. Something so little in our eyes is extremely huge in their eyes.

March 5 – Trust your Instincts

Go with your instinct. Trust your gut. You've got that sixth sense for a reason, use it. If you feel someone is struggling with something, say so and encourage them. The very worst that could possibly happen is that you'll show that person just how much you care about them.

March 6 – Forward Encouragement

Email an encouraging blog post to your friends. If you have something automatically coming to your email or stumble across one, take the time to email it and share with someone you think may appreciate it.

March 7 – Kids that Knock and Ask…Get

Buy from kids that come knocking on your door doing fundraisers. If these kids take the time to go door to door, then honor that work. Chances are they have heard "no" from the last 8 houses. It is discouraging and frustrating to experience this. Find something cheap that they have or give up your coffee/lunch for a week and let that money support their cause.

March 8 – No Strings

Give a lottery ticket to a friend in a card with NO strings attached

March 9 – Smooth Pick Me Up

Give a soft touch. Give some nice smelly good lotion to someone who needs a pick me up. Pack it in a cute basket with some ribbon and a nice card letting them know you were thinking of them.

March 10 – Happy Chuck Norris Day

Celebrate Chuck Norris Day! March 10th is Chuck Norris's Birthday. Celebrate BIG, have fun and make it memorable for your family. Have knock 'em dead chicken wings, or round house KICK style chili that packs a punch. For dessert, man up to a HUGE bowl of ice cream or hot fudge sundae. Put as many scoops of ice cream in a HUGE bowl as you can. Add your favorite toppings and pass out the spoons! Watch the eyes of your family light up as you celebrate Big! Make sure you share your favorite Chuck Norris jokes!

March 11 – Color is Beautiful

Send gel pens and stationary to someone who loves to write cards. I know several people who love sending cards and getting them too. When you see cards and pens on sale, grab some for them. Make the pens colorful so they can express themselves "brightly." This gift gives to more than the recipient. Those receiving the heartfelt cards will also have smiles brought their way. This is such a thoughtful gift, in more ways than one.

March 12 - Celebrate

Celebrate the DAY with your guy/gal! Make it special. Candle light, some music and no distractions (none, including cell phone, emails, tweets, texts etc.) will set you up for an amazing evening! This will let them know that your time with them is the most important thing ever! In this hurry up and wait right now world, the slow pace of kindness, joy and love will be a nice change of pace.

March 13 – Stamp are Huge

Postage Stamps are ALWAYS needed! When you purchase a book for yourself, purchase a book for Spreading Joy. We are always sending out foundation requests, thank you notes and the like. This kind of donation will be a HUGE help to our organization!

March 14 – Happiness at your Fingertips

Send encouraging emails to those in your address book. There are so many web sites that have encouraging poems, articles and the like. There is no reason that you can't start an email that will bring smiles to someone sitting down in the morning getting ready to face the day. Especially on Monday! Don't you just hate those Monday emails that start off demanding right away? Send one that starts off with warm fuzzy smiles!

March 15 – Red Cross Needs You

Donate blood. With the natural disasters, community hospitals that are always in need and various other reasons, there is always a need for blood. Seems like a no brainer when you think about it. Easy, peasy, simple. Visit www.redcross.org for blood drives near you.

March 16 – Sincerely Yours

Give sincere compliments today! All day long be aware of the wonderful things about people. Point out the nice smile, great hair day, and nice new purse. Compliment the perfume and glorious smelling cologne that is setting off your smell-o-meter!

March 17 – The Royal Treatment

Get your Princess or Prince out of School early for His/Her Birthday! Celebrate by going for ice cream or something that you normally wouldn't do. Just the 2 of you together will be a wonderful gift of time, laughter and pure joy. Be sure to look into the eyes of the very best gift you have. Make them feel as important as they really are.

March 18 – To Market, To Market

Take the time to shop at your local Farmers Market for fresh fruits and veggies. You'll be helping local people and when you do that you are making a difference for your community.

March 19 – The Journey of Separation is Difficult

Send a card to someone who had a loved one pass away in the last 4-5 months. Let them know you are thinking of them as they are on this new journey without their loved one. It helps to know that someone remembered as well as someone recognizing their loss.

March 20 – Goodie Bags Rule

Make up some goodie bags of half price candy and take them to a nursing home or shelter. After major holidays the candy is wonderfully inexpensive. No one cares when then candy is from. You can even get a huge bowl and put it out at work for others to enjoy. Take advantage of these sales and use them for spreading joy to those around you.

March 21 – Gift Cards, Easy Peasy… Done

Pick up $10.00 McDonald Gift Cards & mail to Spreading Joy. If you picked up two a month all year long, by November you'd be able to mail us 22 precious gift cards that will make a huge difference! Now, imagine if 100 people reading this book did this. Just 100. WOW! Spreading Joy would be giving big at Christmas time with just a few people helping in this fashion.

March 22 – Writing Gratitude

Purchase a journal and colorful pens and give as a gift to a friend. Tie the pens to the front of the wrapped journal. Before wrapping, tuck a note card inside with a few of your favorite quotes and a wish for a glorious day.

March 23 – A Little Extra Goes A Long Way

Give to your local Church! Everyone is hurting financially and when this happens, people tend cut back their giving here. The flip side of this is true as well. When people are hurting and in need, they turn to the church. Don't cut back your giving.

March 24 – Spoil Them

Adopt a Mom/Grandmother and spoil them. Plan monthly dates, send cards for no reason. Call and chit chat while you are doing dishes. Time is one of the greatest gifts ever.

March 25 – Teddy Bears are Softies

Teddy Bears for Seniors! Go to the Dollar Store and buy 20 teddy bears or various stuffed animals and take them to a local Nursing home. Many of these amazing men and women just want someone to spend a few minutes with them each day. This will help with the need of being lonely and give them a way to remember your visit.

March 26 – Time is Precious

Donate your TIME to help your favorite charity! All charities need help. I need people that will email, send thank you cards and search out for products, places to speak and other items. Email me

March 27 – Behind the Counter

Do you frequent a local convenient store each morning for coffee? You see the same workers each morning? Why not surprise them with biscuits from a local fast food place? Your thoughtfulness will surprise them and create a great start to your day.

March 28 – Others, Matter of the Heart

Focus on OTHERS today! Do things for as many people as you can. I believe that if you take the time to plan this out that you could make a difference for 20 to 30 people in one day. Try it and see how it goes. I mean really, how horrible would it be to ONLY make a difference for 18 people instead of 30?

March 29 – Gadgets are Great

Are you a gadget geek? Get the newest versions of the latest thing? Don't let the others just sit and gather dust! Got the latest greatest laptop and not sure what to do with your older one? Donate to Spreading Joy and we will make sure some awesome people are blessed by it.

March 30 – Music in the Mail

Send the gift of music. Send an iTunes gift card to someone as a surprise. Don't even let them know that it's coming. Just drop it in the mail and know that you are sending a huge smile with your delivery.

March 31 – I Wish I had Known

Mentor someone just starting a business, ministry etc. Give them a list of "When I started out, I wish I had known…." and encourage them while they are getting started. This will provide more joy than you can possibly imagine. You have a million questions and no one to ask them to. You wonder if you can do it, the doubts will fly and deep within your heart, you are fearful. Just a little affirmation can carry an individual a very long way. The time saved of struggling to get started; the security of having someone to turn to and the friendship that will be developed along the way is priceless.

nuggetsofJOY:

➤ *Failure is never final, it's usually a detour. Enjoy the new scenery! ~ Marie Wikle*

➤ *A leader is a dealer in hope.--Napoleon Bonaparte*

➤ *Blessed are those who can laugh at themselves, for they shall never cease to be amused.—Unknown*

➤ *Kind words can be short and easy to speak, but their echoes are truly endless.--Mother Teresa*

➤ *We don't stop playing because we grow old; we grow old because we stop playing.--George Bernard Shaw*

April

Emerson said "Scatter Joy." Personally, I think he was on to something Huge! When we enter April, we think of the little rhyme "April showers bring May flowers." Imagine what you'll have a hand in bringing when you are spreading joy.

Sprinkling acts of joy throughout the day is certain to bring about positive attitudes, mile wide smiles and hearts that are touched for all eternity. Have fun bringing about the gorgeous, vibrant May flowers of joy.

April 1 – JEST fooling

APRIL'S Fool! No fooling, make a donation towards Christmas Joy already. Start early, planning ahead and donating something each month towards Christmas will go a long way towards helping so many that are very needy during such a special time of year.

April 2 – Hoppiness Abounds

Purchase Easter candy for neighborhood children. Sure, they will get baskets of candy soon, but really, can you ever have enough Easter Candy?

April 3 – Where History Lives

Volunteer in a Nursing home. When you volunteer and learn your responsibilities you also will learn the residents. This is where history lives! Speaking to them, looking them in the eye, listening to them when your duties afford you time will flood their soul with joy and splash your heart at the same time. The relationship that you'll build will linger in your heart long after your friend has moved on from the nursing home.

April 4 – Listing the Little Things

Start jotting down the million blessings that come your way, your favorite things and the little things that make your life big. Put them in a blog for all to see. Put them on FaceBook or the other various Social Media sites. Publish it somewhere and that alone will encourage others to do the same. Who knows, you may remind someone of many little things in their life that are really HUGE.

April 5 – Let Them Eat Cake

Make a cake for no reason! Enjoy the sweet treat with your family. The good thing about baking is birthdays, anniversaries and such are not required. Cake is always a wonderful treat for anyone, anytime of the year. When is the last time you took a cake right out of the oven, sliced it and topped it with chocolate icing? I remember doing this for someone and the wow factor was pretty cool. Any time they had eaten a cake, it had always cooled first.

April 6 – Shhhhh, No telling

Pick someone and be their secret pal for a week. You can choose someone close by or someone from your online world. Plan ahead, get the address and send something every day. Don't sign it...just do it!

April 7 – Let Me Count The Ways

Tell those that you love, you love them. Seriously. Go on....I'll wait. You can never, ever – ever do this enough. We are not promised tomorrow. We are not promised the next breath. This is one act of joy that you should not be stingy with. Express your love and appreciation often.

April 8 – Labor Day Play

Send your mom flowers on YOUR birthday and have the card say "Happy *Labor* Day" - Get it? L-A-B-O-R Day? She will be so surprised and who knows, it may even take her a moment to figure out the card and what it means. If anything, you'll have a great laugh with her and have made her day special all over again.

April 9 – Reading is Easy Listening

Purchase some audio books that are on CD's for Seniors in a nursing home that are having trouble with their site! Many would love to be able to read, but simply can't see anymore. The joy and thrill of being able to have their book come to life will be something they look forward to day after day.

April 10 – Chronic Pain

Know someone dealing with chronic pain and many physical issues? Give a handwritten note of encouragement. Even if on plain notebook paper, this gesture will warm hearts for days to come. This will give them something tangible to hold on to during times of deep sorrow, pain or loneliness. Chronic pain sufferers are simply grateful that someone recognizes their pain and cares enough to show that they care.

April 11 – Comfort Food
Make extra chili and cornbread muffins. You know good and well that when you are making a batch of Chili, that you make entirely too much! This is a good problem to have as it provides you with an opportunity to make a difference and spread a little joy. Put the extra in a nice container that can be thrown away, package up the muffins in a cute little basket that can be kept and take to a neighbor. The delight of a wonderful hot meal as well as not having to cook for an evening will be evident in their mile wide smile!

April 12 – Oh Bother

Everyone feels like "what's the use" sometimes. We get bombarded with the Eeyore (from Winnie the Pooh) symptoms and can't shake them. You can help. Let those that are important to you know they are important! Is it a best friend that you need to reach out to? Is it a child or spouse? Is it someone online that is always there for you? Tell them. Send a card, send an email or make that call. If they matter to you, tell them so. This will help remind their hearts that they truly do make a difference.

April 13 – Merry Un-Birthday

Do something extra nice for someone whose Birthday is NOT today. Don't just purchase a gift for them, but make a donation towards his favorite charity or yours. Make a difference for someone and honor them at the same time.

April 14 – Eggsalent Idea

Give Reese's Eggs today! These are simply some of the best candies on the face of the earth. I think it's because there is more peanut butter in these little gems than there are the regular Reese's Cups. There's no wrong way to give a Reese's Egg.

April 15 – Ordinary People Need You

Get gifts for others today. Pick up 2 or 3 things for someone that you do not know. It could be someone at a nursing facility, it could be a cashier at your local grocery store or it could be the bank teller that you see each week. Whomever you choose, you are sure to turn their ordinary day into a spectacular day!

April 16 – Fastest Way to a Man's Heart

Buy a couple of cakes and take to a men's shelter. Who doesn't love cake? We all do and many times, this is not something that a shelter will splurge on. This is such a sweet treat for some guys that will not be expecting much of anything at all.

April 17 – The Cutest Little Princess

Purchase some fingernail polish and put it in a cute little bag. Take these bags to a local homeless or women's shelter for the little girls that will be coming through. They are already scared and out of their comfort zone, so this comforting thing will help to ease their fears.

April 18 – Bake Off

Have everyone sign up to make the most delicious dessert ever and have a contest to see who has the best. To sample each dessert and be able to vote, charge a small admission of about $3.00 and then donate the money to your favorite charity or right here to Spreading Joy. Compile the recipes and distribute them to your employees to use at home. This sweet idea will benefit so many people!

April 19 – Dipping Fun

Plan a sweet break by dipping cookies or other items into chocolate. With a microwave and candy melts, you can dip pretzels, cookies, strawberries and much more for a time of sharing, laughter and fun. This is so easy, even small children love getting in on the fun.

April 20 - $5 Bucks is MORE than $5 Bucks

When sending a card to encourage someone, tuck a $5.00 bill inside. I personally have received this some a special lady several times and she blesses my heart each time. I generally make sure that I use it for "me" instead of giving it away or doing something else. Then I would take the time to not only thank her but tell her of the special treat she provided for me.

April 21 – Serving up Loads of Love

Volunteer at a local shelter. Men or Women's shelters are always looking for people to help out with many needs. There is always something to do there.

April 22 – Double Fun

Making cookies for your family? Double the recipe and take to work and share! What a wonderful treat this would make, especially on a Friday or even a Monday when no one truly wants to be there.

April 23 – Feeding Frenzy

Feed the meters! Go for it, have fun and make a difference.

April 24 – Final Gift Lives On

Are you an organ donor? If not.....why not? Let the last thing you do make a world of difference for someone. This simple act will have a huge ripple effect. The friends and family of the recipient will be forever grateful for your amazing generosity.

April 25 – Help the History Makers

Seek out the elderly in your neighborhood and do yard work for them. They cannot take care of things as they once could. If you have time, strike up a conversation with them and not only will you make a difference to them, you'll also walk away with some wonderful bits of history that many may not know about.

April 26 – Good Sticky Stuff

Leave a sticky note of encouragement on a few of your co-workers computer. Don't sign it. Just do it. Even add a quote if you have time. If you can draw or are a doodler, dress it up! Add a touch of flair, a little of the brightness that is in your heart and you'll add great joy to their day.

April 27 – Half Off is Wonderful

Half price Easter candy is such a wonderful way share the deliciousness of chocolate! There are so many places that can benefit from this wonderful gift. Shelters, women's homes, kids programs at various churches. This act of joy is half price for you and a special treat for them.

April 28 – I Positively Agree

End on a positive note. I realize this cannot always be accomplished, but it is worth the effort. Especially if you are leaving your family for a trip or work, make sure your last words are positive ones.

April 29 – Plastic Bag Overload

Do you find yourself overrun with plastic bags even though you use them for nearly everything? Take them with you and reuse them, or better yet, purchase several bags to take with you each time you shop. Keep them in your trunk, all stuffed inside of one bag so that you'll always have them handy. Doing this can have you saying so long plastic bags in no time.

April 30 – Children are Awesome Heroes, Empower them

Help your child(ren) complete an act of joy every day. Starting joyful habits at a young age will instill a desire for kindness that will last a life time. Some children are givers by nature. Nurture this gift. For those that are not, point out opportunities and make a difference with them.

NuggetsofJOY:

> ➤ *Be a light in someone's life today, no matter how small - you'll still light up their world! ~ Marie Wikle*
> ➤ *Always bear in mind that your own resolution to succeed is more important than any other thing.--Abraham Lincoln*
> ➤ *There are hundreds of languages in the world, but a smile speaks them all.—Anonymous*
> ➤ *Sometimes your joy is the source of your smile, but sometimes your smile can be the source of your joy. - Thich Nhat Hanh*
> ➤ *Words are potent weapons for all causes, good or bad.--Manly Hall*

May

Another month of ideas that will brighten your day, lift your spirits and have your heart splashing in joy as you are making a difference for others. Fun, colorful and often simple, these acts of joy will have your days and nights filled with inspiration.

When the inspiration hits, use that to motivate someone to step up and reach out to others.   You'll have just as much fun watching someone make a difference as you do when you are actively participating yourself.

May 1 – Don't Be Green With Envy

Be happy for someone else's success AND help them, in any way, shape or form to be successful. Tell the truth. This can be hard sometimes as we wonder when it will be our time. We all want success, but it doesn't always come in the way we'd like it too. This is sure to lift your heart and inspire the one you are encouraging. Go for it! Inspire!

May 2 – One Lump or Two

Host an afternoon Tea Party with your child(ren). These will be cherished memories indeed. Before you know it, you'll be attending the wedding of your princess. Don't take this time for granted! Remember, PINKIES up!

May 3 – Brighten Someone's Corner

Pick flowers from your garden and give away. If you have a green thumb and enjoy the rewards of your garden, imagine how someone with OUT a green thumb would enjoy a vase full of your beautiful flowers. This act of joy will last in someone's home or on their desk for days. Bonus joy – when they look upon the flowers, they will think of you and smile!

May 4 - Let Grumpy Sleep

Do not wake up Grumpy. Let him sleep. (hahahahaha. Ok, that is as old as the hills, but still funny to me.) Seriously. If you wake up grumpy, focus on others, think of the millions of little things that make YOUR life big and keep the ickiness to yourself until it passes. We want to be spreadingJOY not spreadingICK. On my web site there is an article called Confessions of a Cranky Gal. Check it out. See how some online friends, Little Debbie Cakes and a message from Little Debbie made the crankies just ooze away.

May 5 – Don't Waste Unused Miles

Share your frequent flyer miles. Do you travel often? Do you have an abundance of miles racked up? Offer a night or 2 at a hotel to someone. Purchase a magazine subscription for someone. Let me know that you would be a resource of miles for Spreading JOY. Endless ways of spreading joy here!

May 6 – Selfless

Use a gift card that you received for someone else! Wow. Think about this act of joy for a moment. HOW selfless is this? You'll make a difference and it will not have cost YOU a single cent. Go for it! Let your heart be flooded with joy as you give of yourself!

May 7 – Your UN-Birthday

Celebrate your UN-Birthday with your family. Make a cake from scratch, using basic ingredients from the pantry. Get everyone involved. The fun, laughter and the fact that it's your UN-birthday will have your home filled with great laughter and JOY!

May 8 – Everyone Loves Free

List some items in the FREE section of Craig's List that you don't need any longer. This will help people who need a break and free up some much needed space in your home.

May 9 – I Just Called To Say…

Phone calls – for NO reason. Love this. Go ahead and make that call. You never know who you will encourage, whose day you'll make brighter and how that person just might have needed that encouragement at just that moment. When someone just "pops" into my mind out of nowhere, I generally take that as a sign that I need to contact them and make sure everything is ok and then spend some time just talking with them. Besides, who doesn't love phone calls for no reason? Right?

May 10 - Flowers for the Unsuspecting

Take flowers to a hospital and give to someone who hasn't had visitors. Believe it or not, there are people in the hospital who never get visitors or phone calls, much less flowers. You'll lift their spirits in ways untold!

May 11 – Awareness is Key

When singing in the car, LOUDLY, be aware of the feelings of others – if YOU are not alone. ;) Make sure its songs they can sing along to. This is just a common sense act of joy because for some people who love singing, common sense just flies out the window and the singing can't be stopped.

May 12 – Such a Cute Little Baby

Know a new Mom and Baby? Take a complete meal to them, along with some disposable plates and utensils. This will help make the first few days of adjusting to having a baby in the house easier as well as save time on clean up. You will have touched this mom's heart by giving her some much needed rest and support.

May 13 – Time to Par-taaay!

Attend the party. Seriously, you were invited. The Host is working hard at putting it together! YOU will make someone happy...so GO – have fun, sit back and ENJOY! You may meet up with some friends you have not seen in a while. Be prepared to laugh and have a wonderful time. *Personal Note* - Today is my Brother's Birthday! I'm definitely going to enjoy HIS party! **Happy Birthday John!** Love you.

May 14 – Jars Aplenty

Do you have several of the larger jars just hanging around waiting to be used? Why not use them for some staples that you have in your pantry? Use them for gifts. Why not put popcorn kernels in one, spaghetti broken in half in another and miniature Reese's Cups in yet another. Add a cute cloth topper to the jar of goodies and give as a gift. The possibilities are endless!

May 15 – Extra Household Items

Donate household items to someone in need. You have tons of dishes that you do not use; you have extra glasses, bowls and such. Find a young couple that could benefit from these items and ask if they need extra.

May 16 – HALT!

SLOW down – so you won't be grouchy! YOU know it's true. When you are in a hurry every SINGLE thing gets on your nerves and you are grouchy. (Pointing the finger at MYSELF!! I never do things slowly.) It never fails! You are in a hurry and if it can go wrong and slow you down, it will. So, stay a step ahead of the game and pace yourself.

May 17 – Dessert First Please

Eat Dessert FIRST. You will be a huge spreadingJOY hero to your family when you plan this. Go all out – do ice cream in waffle bowls. Have Reese's Cup Pie (and invite me over) or Chocolate Cake with Chocolate frosting. Have it first and have lots of fun! Imagine the eyes of your children as you call them to the table and that wonderful bowl of ice cream is sitting there waiting on them. You'll have a memory that will last a life time in the heart of your family!

May 18 – Forgiveness Is Key

Be forgiving today. Bury the hatchet and let bygones, be bygones. This will do more than spread joy to the person you are forgiving, it will free your heart from the bondage that harboring un-forgiveness brings. Let it go and free yourself as well.

May 19 – So Sneaky

Write a note for your child(ren) expressing how proud of them you are. Leave it on their pillow or put it in their overnight bag. This is always fun for a lunch box too, especially if your child is young.

May 20 – Moms Are the Greatest

Happy Birthday Mommie! Do something fun for your Mom for her birthday. If you are fortunate enough to have her with you still, send her something fun, unusual and totally stupendous.

Think outside the box as flowers and chocolates are wonderful, but give her something that she will laugh about, remember fondly and treasure in her heart for years to come. Take her to a place on her wish list. Make it fun, fabulous and filled with things that will remind her just how wonderful she truly is. Mom...I sure do love you!

May 21 – Dream With Me

Have a family meal at the table. Talk about current events in the family. Talk about dreams for the future, for your children's future. Talk about your bucket lists and try to do one or two things from that list each summer.

May 22 – Smell the Roses

Take time to smell the roses. You pass them in the store, you pass them in gardens. Take the time to do it. If you are to busy to stop and smell the sweet fragrances of some roses and other flowers, then you are much to busy. I understand that sometimes you have to hurry in and out, but not every single time. You never know who is watching and how you will inspire them.

May 23 - *Wink*

Wink at random people. Make sure you pass along a huge smile too! Seriously, how awesome is it to be minding your own business and someone smiles at you and then before you leave gives a wink & even a nod. Simply awesome!

May 24 – One Size Fits All

Give gift certificate to your best friend for their birthday! Add in a personal note telling them why they are the greatest friend in the world! The few moments you take to put into writing why your best friend is the bestest ever, will last on their hearts for a life time.

May 25 – Assumptions Are Usually Wrong

Do not assume – Don't do it. What you think you might know isn't necessarily the truth of the actual known fact. You just never know….you know? Don't group people by where they live, how they dress or the size they are. Don't assume that just because someone is from a certain city or country that they are like all the others you've met. Don't assume.

May 26 – Smiling Eyes

Give time to your spouse or significant other. Go out together, to a book store, park and spend some time together. Walk the trails of a nearby park area. Rummage through some books and or magazines at a book store. Look into their eyes and smile!

May 27 – Return The Favor

Return a favor – without being asked. You have no idea how wonderful this truly is unless someone has seen a need you have and without your prompting have helped to meet that need. This is a priceless act that the heart will hang on to for years to come.

May 28 – Extra Extra!!!

Extra smiles and kindness for someone in distress, feeling teary or extremely emotional about something. Even if you don't know them, take a moment to smile and remind them that it WILL be alright. Don't make light of their situation, but do be encouraging. If you've been fortunate enough to have this happen to you, then I don't need to tell you how awesome this act of joy is!

May 29 – Bratty, Joyfully So

Sometimes we simply don't feel good. Sometimes all we want to do is just sleep the sickness away. That should be a red flag to step back, rest and pay attention to the signal your body is sending out. REST! If you have to be out and about when you aren't feeling good, and that results in feeling a little bratty, do it with joy.

May 30 – Boost Confidence

Share confidence! Remind others that they CAN do this. They are excellent at what they do. They are strong and will make it through. This kind of confidence can help someone take the next step into what they feel may be a journey of uncertainty. Spoken with love and tenderness, you may help them to move past the fears that are holding them back.

May 31 – Thank You Service Men and Women

Our Military - Shake hands or somehow, some way greet our wonderful Military personnel each and every time you see someone in uniform. Look them in the eyes and say thank you. Make this a rule! I never pass up this opportunity. There have been times that I've had a few extra dollars and have been able to purchase their meal and/or dessert. Go the extra mile for these modern day heroes.

nuggetsofJOY:

> - *Infect others with Joy! Those smiles that you give away are powerful for the heart that is discouraged. ~ Marie Wikle*
> - *You have to sniff out joy. Keep your nose to the joy trail. – Buffy Sainte-Marie*
> - *If you can keep your head when all about you are losing theirs, it's just possible you haven't grasped the situation.--Jean Kerr*
> - *Nothing is so strong as gentleness, and nothing is so gentle as true strength.--Ralph Sockman*
> - *Impossible situations can become possible miracles.--Robert H. Schuller*

June

Sticks and stones may break my bones, but words will never hurt me…. WRONG – do you hear me on this? WORDS are so very powerful. You can change the world for someone by using a few simple encouraging words. On the flip side of that, you can cause someone's world to come crashing in on them by being reckless with your words.

ENCOURAGE someone today!

June 1 – Yard Sales

Hold a yard sale and donate half of the proceeds to Spreading Joy Corporation. For a few hours of work, your pocketbook will have some extra green, your home a little less clutter and your heart flooded with joy as you donate half of the proceeds to make a difference.

June 2 – Double Benefits

Go to yard sales and buy things. People are selling for a reason! You never know what treasures are there waiting for you. You'll find books, stuffed animals for the younger children, frames, sweaters etc. You will get some great deals as well as help the person who is hosting the yard sale. People are downsizing and doing whatever they need to do to make things easier for themselves financially. Have fun and happy exploring!

June 3 – Singing in the Rain

You remember what it was like playing in the sprinklers as a child, right? Well, how about playing in the biggest sprinklers of all…the SKY! Play in the rain! Sounds simply crazy don't it? It's refreshingly wonderful! You'll HAVE to let me know when you do this!

June 4 – Firefighters are Awesome Heroes

Support our Firefighters! Do something special for your local Fire House. The guys and gals there will be so thrilled that you took the time to visit as well as will be thankful for the special item you bring them.

June 5 – Give Others A Hand

Be generous with the pat on the backs, the handshakes and eye to eye contact. Positive reinforcement here! No need to worry if anyone will appreciate this act of JOY or not, because when you are looking into their eyes, you'll know – instantly!

June 6 – Surprise Movie Tickets

Buy a movie ticket for the person/couple in line behind you. When you've told the cashier what you want to see and it's time to pay for your ticket, simply turn to the people behind you and say, I'm spreading joy and I'd like to purchase your tickets for you. Can you imagine their surprise and delight? Try it and see just how much this will make their night.

June 7 – Dad's Make the World Go Round

Happy Father's Day! Tell those guys close to you just how important they are and if you are lucky enough to still have your Father with you, then make HIS day so very special! A note inside a gorgeous card telling him WHY you love him and WHY you are thankful that he is your father will be better than any gift that money can buy. Steal a few extra hugs today too. One can never have enough hugs from their father.

June 8 – Dinner Guest

Invite someone who is alone, such as a widow(er) over for dinner. They will enjoy the company, good food and hospitality and you'll be amazed at the history and great stories you'll be privileged to hear.

June 9 – Help Ease the Discomfort

Do you know a Cancer Survivor? Tell them you appreciate them and just how thankful you are that they are a part of your life! Do you know someone who is currently going through chemo? Why not go by and sit with them for a portion of their time. If you have time, stay with them the entire day. Remember laughter is good medicine.

June 10 – You Are Coming With Me

Kidnap a friend or stay at home mom for a few hours this evening. Treat them to their favorite meal, drink or dessert. Have fun, walk around a mall or park and simply enjoy the gift of time with each other.

June 11 – Kind Words are Never Ending

Give kind words freely. Honestly, after a day of "you didn't accomplish this, you made a D on that test, you monthly projections were off by a long shot…blah, blah, blah" WE all need to hear more positive things that we *did* do. Kind words will build and strengthen something so deep within the person receiving them that you may never realize the extent of the encouragement you were to them.

June 12 – Rain, Rain…Go Away…NO…WAIT!!

Love plants? I do too. Leave a few containers outside and collect rainwater to water them with the rainwater. Talk about simple!

June 13 – Thanks Mom and Dad

Write your parents a note letting them know why they are so very special. We tend to just think that our parents will always be there. It doesn't matter how old you are, if your parent is still alive and with you, take some time right now and write out that note! It will be the best gift you give them!

June 14 – Experience is Priceless

Hire a recently graduated Senior. In this day you have to have experience to get hired. Well, this is a problem for many high school seniors as they are looking for their first job. Hire them and then mentor and mold them into the best employee you have. You never know where this will lead your company or how this will affect the leadership skills of the kid you hired.

June 15 – Good Morning Sunshine

Surprise your family with a HOT breakfast one morning, instead of the traditional quick milk, juice and cereal as they are running out of the door. Get up a little earlier, start the delicious food and the aromas will sneak into everyone's room and tap on their taste buds! Your gift of time in preparing this delicious meal will help them float through the day, facing each turn with a smile!

June 16 – Bring On Friday

TGIF -I love Fridays! Make some lemonade for neighbors and/or road crew people. When the sun is bright this thirst quencher will delight the taste buds and hearts of those you think to share with.

June 17 – 2nd Hand Treasures

Buy super cheap baby items at a 2nd hand store and give to women's shelter. They always have people transitioning in and out of their facility and can use these items.

June 18 – Thank for Teaching With Your Heart

Give a note to a Sunday School Teacher (or school teacher) that made a difference in your life. Technology makes it so easy to find people. The lasting effect in their heart will make the time you spend finding them worth it. You can search while you are watching your favorite TV show.

June 19 – Reading Is Fun

Recently read a book that you loved? Has a friend given you a book that they had published? Write a review and post it without being asked to on your web site promoting it. Every bit of promotion helps. Every kind and positive review will help to spread the word about their success. Use your voice for others.

June 20 – Starry Delights

Shoot for the stars...give Cosmic Brownies from Little Debbie

June 21 – Peanutty Deliciousness

Make some homemade peanut butter cookies and take some to some of the elderly neighbors that live down the road from you. Share the cookies with the neighborhood kids. Simply share!

June 22 – An Unexpected Finish

While having Sunday lunch, send dessert to a table nearby. Pay attention to when they are getting close to finishing and have the waiter deliver 2 of their best desserts. Send one chocolaty and one not, just in case someone doesn't like chocolate. (I can NOT imagine not liking chocolate, but personally know a few people who don't.)

June 23 – A World of Do-Gooders

Point out those do-gooders you come in contact with. Go the extra mile to encourage the "encouragers" in your life. EVERYONE needs to be encouraged! Everyone!

June 24 – While You Were Out

If you have someone's Instant Message or Skype contact info, leave them a message even if they are off line. They will find it and be encouraged when they log on. This is really easy for those of your contacts that live in various time zones. Figure out when they are sleeping and leave them a message.

June 25 – Proms Are Special

Donate your old Prom Dress to a facility that will give them to girls that are not able to purchase one for their self. Many young ladies dream of a wonderful prom night but will not be able to attend due to the lack of funds needed to purchase a dress.

June 26 – Double Deliciousness

When making homemade bread, double the recipe and give some away. I think gifts from the kitchen are simply delicious, as they are always sprinkled with love.

June 27 – What?

Listen today, really stop and listen.

June 28 – Sudden Down Pours

Summer thunder storms are horrible so carry an extra umbrella and give it to a poor soul in need. I usually never carry an umbrella. I don't know why, I just never have. I can't tell you how many times I've been rescued by someone letting me walk under their umbrella with them. If I'm only heading home or no place in particular, it's not a problem as I love walking in the rain. But for those few times when I've needed an umbrella hero, I'm so thankful for those kind hearts.

June 29 – Text Me

Send an encouraging text to let someone know you were thinking of them. With the availability of unlimited texting and so many great quotes and creative minds, this is such an easy way of making a heart smile!

June 30 – Back 2 School Rocks

Support Spreading Joy's Back to School Project. We strive to give away as many back packs filled with school supplies as possible each and every year. Maybe you can initiate a Matching Grant of $1000.00 stating that all donations will be matched up to $1000.00? Perhaps you can make a onetime gift to help or you know someone who has back packs and can donate several hundred to us. If you can't do any of these items, then consider emailing everyone in your email list about our Back to School event. Spreading the word can be very effective as your contacts are not always the same as anyone else's.

nuggetsofJOY:

> ➤ *WE have resources that NO one else has. We can make a powerful difference right here, right now. ~ Marie Wikle*
> ➤ *You must do the thing you think you cannot do.--Eleanor Roosevelt*
> ➤ *Be more concerned with your character than your reputation, because your character is what you really are, while your reputation is merely what others think you are.--John Wooden*
> ➤ *Appreciation can make a day--even change a life, Your willingness to put it into words is all that is necessary.--Margaret Cousins*
> ➤ *The best and most beautiful things in the world cannot be seen or even touched. They must be felt with the heart.--Helen Keller*

July

Whether it is vacations or Staycations, you have an abundance of opportunities to be a light in the dark. Take some time to look through the eyes of compassion this month. Refrain from judging, assuming or just being downright crude. Everyone is struggling with something. Just because we can't see it, it doesn't mean it's not there. Any kind of light in the darkness has a great affect. Instead of just flickering like a candle, be a beacon! Stand tall, like a lighthouse, warning others of the dangers of discouragement and selfishness.

July 1 – e-mail A Difference

Email the *50 Ways of Making a Difference Without Spending a Penny* list to someone who has a huge heart but is without the financial means to make a difference. Remind them that there are so many ways to make a difference without breaking the bank. Doing what you can, where you are, with what you have – without feeling guilty about it!! THAT is spreading joy!

July 2 – Tipping Allowed

Tip the bagger at the Grocery store. Many places frown on this, but ask them to help you carry your groceries to the car and slide them a tip. How wonderful will this act of joy be?

July 3 - Color Your World

Color with some children; better yet, color with YOUR children. Don't even stay inside the lines. Be adventurous and color outside the lines. Use bold primary colors. Use pastel colors for the grass. Let your inner child run free with your children. That memory will take up so much room in their little hearts for years to come!

July 4 – Celebrate our Freedom

Freedom isn't free and we owe a world of thanks to many men and women that help to keep us safe and our liberties free. Find and treat some of our military to something nice. Make a difference throughout this day for them. Shake hand with government officials including Police, Fire and all Military personnel. They matter and need to know it.

July 5 – Plan, Laugh and Chat

Invite a friend over for coffee, dessert and a fun time of chatting. Try and just let your cares sit outside the door. Laugh, remember, plan and even explore future adventures. Above all, laugh!

July 6 – See a Penny, Pick It Up...

Drop some quarters at the park or parking lot, kids will love finding them! Can you imagine their joy as they are walking along to a store they don't want to go into and see a shiny quarter waiting for them? Or running through a park having a blast and see some money on the ground. You could go a little bigger if you can afford it and take 10 $1.00 bills and just scatter them in places.

July 7 – Free From Daily Chores

 Establish a monthly "NO Chore Day" for your entire family. Mom – yes, this includes you too. Make sure you do something fun with that time. The dishes will wait for you!

July 8 – Shirts for the Homeless

Keep extra t-shirts in car for homeless. If it's the winter time this is especially handy. You never know when you'll be able to brighten someone's day with such a simple little gesture.

July 9 – Speak your Peace

Write a review or leave me a comment about this book or with ideas of spreading joy without spending a penny. I will be glad to site the source in future publications!

July 10 – Breakfast for the Workplace

TGIF - take biscuits to work this Friday! What a way to celebrate the end of the week. Purchase a dozen sausage biscuits and enjoy your morning coffee with this delicious treat. Ok, so chances are it's not a Friday. Take breakfast anyway!

July 11 – Don't Toss, Donate

Donate your used computer, projectors etc to someone that doesn't have one. You may have to take some time to research it, but it will be completely worth it. There are many single moms who would love NOT to have to go to a public library to use the internet.

July 12 – Take Time to Laugh

Make someone laugh - really laugh. Regardless of the good, the bad, or the ugly take some time to just sit, remember, giggle and laugh. Have fun just being relaxed and remembering. If you are a good joke teller, then tell away. If you are not, then tell away and then enjoy the laughter as well. There is nothing like laughing till the tears come and you can hardly catch your breath.

July 13 – Children Love Spreading Joy

Include your Children in Spreading Joy so that it will become a lifelong habit. Start when they are tiny by asking them to pick something out for someone else. You are not just teaching sharing habits, you are teaching them to take their eyes off of themselves for a bit and to focus on someone else. Take them with you when you help the homeless or volunteer at a nursing center. Raising givers is not impossible.

July 14 – Facebook Helps Spread the Word

Post Links to Charity organizational events to your facebook wall or twitter feed. If you can't donate a financial gift, donate your voice! Do it daily to help promote the event without being asked to. We live in a day and age where our voice has more reach than we've ever had before. Using technology, emails and our web sites, we can help spread the word about events and charities that are near and dear to our hearts. Stand up and SHOUT! Your heart will be flooded with great joy when you do!

July 15 – Love the Little Things

Be aware of your surroundings. Something as simple as holding the door and smiling at the person going out can make a difference in their day. Don't discount the little things. They are huge!

July 16 – Thank You For Calling

Make every phone call extremely pleasant. Even the "Non helping" help desk calls. Sure you can be frustrated with how long it takes someone to help you from the support center. I know many phone calls can be annoying, but if you focus on spreading joy, you'll be able to do this easily.

July 17 - Shopping Helps Others

If you shop Amazon.com USE the affiliate link of a friend! WHY not let a small percentage of your purchase help someone? Don't know anyone? Let me know and I'll help direct you!

July 18 – Tips Bring Smiles

Give the bus boy $5.00 -They need a little help too! Sometimes we see them helping out the waitress and I know they get some of the tips, but still. What a wonderful surprise for him to have someone "notice" the great job he does. You are giving more than a tip, you are giving a mile wide smile!

July 19 – Introductions Are Gateways

Introduce yourself to someone you see all the time but do not usually speak to. This scares some people to pieces, but once you make the first move, you'll see that it gets easier after that. You never know, you may develop a lifelong friendship. Now, put on your best smile and head on over to them.

July 20 – Cool Treats

Give Ice Cream Sandwiches to everyone today. This is such a sweet treat, especially on a hot summer day. Many boxes have 12 in them, so you will be making 11 people smile that day. What?!? Not spreading joy to yourself? Nonsense! Have one too!

July 21 – Comments Encourage Writers

Blog Comments – Take a few moments and tell the writer of the article if you liked or even disliked what was written. Feed back is always wonderful! The little bit of time it takes to do this will encourage the writer. Also, if your comments are thought out, you never know what discussion you will spark or where that discussion will lead.

July 22 – Christmas in July

Start planning for CHRISTMAS! Start an "others" box and put gifts for others in it. If you see toys that are normally $10.00 on sale for 3 or 4 bucks each, grab them, put them in your "others box" and by the time Christmas rolls around, you'll have 20-30 toys to help others with! You'll be amazed at how quickly this adds up and how your heart will be swelling with great happiness upon delivery.

July 23 – A Little Click Helps a Lot

Click on Ads when visiting web sites. – You are already there reading & the owner of the site makes some money off each click, so why not?

July 24 – That Was Awesome

Show sincere appreciation. Eye Contact and sincere thanks can turn a horrible day into one where the heart is soaring. Think about a time that someone sincerely complimented you on your work, clothing, eye/hair color etc. Think of how your heart beamed with delight. YOU have this same power to make that happen. Give freely!

July 25 – Great Service = Great Thanks

Write a thank you note on the bill you receive from the waitress. Often times they are blamed for the food not being right, the volume of the facility and so many things that they personally cannot control. Take a moment and jot a note on your bill telling her/him thank you for the extra wonderful service and compliment their awesome smile! You'll never ever know just what a difference you can make in their night. Talk about a pep in their step? This is such an easy way to bring joy to someone's heart.

July 26 – Sew Amazing

Can you sew? Make several blankets to donate. Look for scrap material at yard sales, clearance sales etc. Many times this can be done while watching TV and having fun.

July 27 – Games Night Brings Great Memories

Host a game night with your family – eat dessert first! Turn off cell phones (ok – kids, you can leave yours on….) but spend time laughing together playing games! Remember, it doesn't matter who wins, just enjoy being together and having fun.

July 28 – From Garden to Heart

Give a basket of home grown veggies. So many people are growing their own veggies. I, unfortunately, am not green thumbed enough to do this. If you have a garden, then share with someone. Get a basket, fill it full of your delicious veggies, tuck in a card and then deliver. Simple, yet effective!

July 29 – Homemade Deliciousness

Bake homemade cookies with items you have in your pantry and share with neighborhood children (of ALL ages) Easy recipes such as No flour Peanut Butter Cookies. 1 cup of peanut butter, 1 cup of sugar and 1 egg. Mix and then bake for about 15 – 20 minutes on 320. Oh the peanutty goodness you have when they are done. Just make sure no one is allergic to peanuts!

July 30 – Great Opportunities in Church

Go to Church. There are so many churches to choose from and when people are discouraged, they will attend church more often. You can make a huge difference here. The smiles, handshakes and the hugs will allow you to make new friends, learn about the hearts, trials and tribulations of others and afford you many opportunities of spreading joy.

July 31 – Cool Treats

During the hot summer months, feed the homeless and include some type of popsicle or something cold. This will make a huge difference and will not cost a lot. They will thank you for taking the time to think of adding something to help cool them off.

nuggetsofJOY:

- *A friend hugs the heart, brings smiles through tears & even when apart, is always near! Be that kind of friend today! ~ Marie Wikle*
- *To give without any reward, or any notice, has a special quality of its own.--Anne Morrow Lindbergh*
- *The really great man is the man who makes every man feel great.--G. K. Chesterton*
- *Blessed are those who can give without remembering and take without forgetting.--Melvin Schleeds*
- *For it is in giving that we receive.--St. Francis Of Assisi*

August

I don't know about you, but usually when I reach August, I start wondering where the year went. It seems to fly by quicker with each passing year. I usually start preparing financially for Christmas as well as the meals and such that we'll have as a family. Given the ups and downs of the economy, you can never start too soon. Use this extra reminder to prepare you to be able to give at your heart's delight, without getting into financial trouble.

August 1 – School Time

School Supplies Needed! When back to school draws near, start purchasing those items that will make the first day of school magical for children who think it will be horrible. The difference this will make is incalculable. You are giving them an opportunity to start school with their head held high and a sense of pride. Purchasing some each week to donate will be gentle on the wallet as well as impact their heart.

August 2 – Joyful Volunteer

Volunteer for a cause that is near to your heart. If you enjoy the spirit of the charity, then you'll completely enjoy helping and volunteering. Sometimes volunteering is seen as drudgery but when volunteering for something you are passionate about, the time will fly by and you energizing spirit will be contagious to so many.

August 3 – Simple Words, Lasting Impression

Speak to the elderly you pass. Look them in the eye and smile. We tend to forget about these great individuals who paved the way for us. We hurry through the grocery store, dashing past them, never stopping to see if they would like or need any help. We see them walking slowly in the park and speed around them. Slow down, smile and speak to them. Say thank you for your part in developing our world. Their heart will soar and yours will be flying high as well.

August 4 – Rise Above Negativity

Encourage and uplift those around you! Be positive no matter how you feel. We all have those days where we want to get back in bed and pretend the morning never came. We all want to order up a "do-over" and start fresh, but that is not always possible. What IS possible is not affecting everyone around us with negativity. I'm not telling you to never express your bad times and such, but as a "whiner", sometimes we do tend to go overboard – so, just keep an eye on the negativity.

August 5 – Serve up Sweetness

Do some baking! Bag it up and give it away. Easy as pie! Ok, pie doesn't seem to be that easy, but baking cookies, making homemade candies are so easy with the bazillions of recipes on the internet these days. Get the cute little cellophane bags from the dollar store and give freely!

August 6 – Good Search Gives Back

Instead of "googling" use "Good Search" and give to Spreading Joy! When you search or shop, Good Search.com will give back to the charity of your choice. Many will look at 2% or at the 1 cent that is donated and think that isn't much, but if there were 1,000 of you doing 10 searches a day, then that alone would add up to a huge payout at the end of the year. Don't discount the little things! They are often the best and biggest things!

August 7 – Reading is Priceless

Read with your children and enjoy some great quality time with them. Nothing like being curled up with your child and reading their favorite book that you've read 37 times before.

Before you realize it, you'll blink and you'll be leaving them at college. No longer will you be able to curl up with them and read their favorite book to them. Add in some hot chocolate with marshmallows and you've got a special memory.

August 8 – Buy One GIVE One FREE

Donate your "free items" from the buy one get one free – to a local food pantry. Seriously! You just hit the gold mine on the BOGO free offers. Why not take the freebies to the homeless shelter down the road or to the food pantry at your local Church? We didn't spend any money on it. There will be other freebies, so for once this year, or once a month how ever long you can, buy one and give the free one away. You'll be glad you did.

August 9 – Children Love Making a Difference

Help your child to do one kindness a day for someone. Starting this for them when they are young will help them to be more sensitive to making a difference for others. Their awareness for little things and just how easy it is to make a difference will serve them well as an adult. Start now and watch what a giving person your child grows into.

August 10 - Pizzalicious

Celebrate the weekend by ordering a large pizza or 2 for someone and have it delivered. This is such a cool thing! Make sure the person(s) is home before ordering. Be sure you call the person that will be receiving the pizza about 10 minutes before time and let them know they have a "gift" coming, to just accept it. Love the weekends for doing special things for special people.

August 11 – Helping Hands At the Hospital

Volunteer at a hospital. There are so many things you can do at a hospital. So many people need the warm smile. They need the kind, gentle voice and the reassurance that "it's" all going to be ok. You may just deliver magazines or help people get from point A to point B. Doing this with a smile will make a difference to countless people!

August 12 - Sincerely Grateful

Say Thank you and mean it. Many times we just say thank you because it's a natural reaction. Take the time to say it and say why you are thankful. Those words will linger on the recipient's heart for days.

August 13 – Grrrrr

Be Patient today. Ok, I'm YELLING this to myself. So many things just get under our skin and the shoulda, woulda and coulda's are never ending. The "ToDo" list keeps growing and our patience with others wears thin. Especially so with those we love the most. Keep it under wraps today. You'll be glad you did.

August 14 – Used Clothing is a Life Saver for Some

Donate gently used clothing. I like to look for places that not only sell the clothing, but will give them away to needy families. There is a Christian Ministries near our house that will give families 30 or so articles of clothing for each family member, per season. In this economy, many people can't afford the luxury of clothing and this is always a huge help.

August 15 – Clearance Items Rule

Clearance Back 2 School items - get them! Save them for next year and then give them to help send children back to school with their head held high! This is so near and dear to my heart. I would love to help thousands and thousands of children to never, ever feel shame in going back to school. We can do this! We can make a difference here!

August 16 – Happy Birthday Dad

Give $20.00 to a random person or your favorite charity in honor or memory of your Father. I do this every August 16th because my dad always carried around a few extra $20.00 bills and if someone needed anything, he would simply give it, expecting nothing in return.

Happy Birthday Dad. I miss you.

August 17 – Give Managers a Smile

Seek out the Grocery Store Manager and let them know what an excellent employee your grocery bagger or cashier was. I love when these guys are friendly. You know after they've been on their feet for hours something like this happening will lift their spirits and help them to make it through the rest of the day. Do not pass up this opportunity to bring smiles to both the employee and the manager.

August 18 – College is Hard on Moms

Encourage Moms that are taking their child to college and leaving them! This is such a hard thing. We know that day is coming; we prepare them to go and be successful. What we tend to forget to do is prepare our own heart to watch them go and be amazing as they journey down a new path that does not include us every day. We are so happy and proud of them, yet many times we cannot contain the tears that flow because we miss them.

August 19 – Hospice Helps Many

Volunteer with Hospice and care for others. This is such a special group. Having been on the receiving end of these giving people, I'm amazed at how calming, soothing and helpful they truly are. This is such a hard time for many and these people know how to help us without making us feeling worse than we already do.

August 20 – Thank a Teacher

Write a thank you note to your child's teacher. Teachers are among those that I consider unsung Heroes. Normally they are used to only hearing the bad, the "not my child," the anger from the kids. The pay isn't the greatest, so they are in it to make a difference. Why not return the favor? Why not take the time to write a note and thank the hero in your child's life this year? You never know how special that card will be to your child's teacher.

August 21 – Classroom Reading

Volunteer to read to a class at your local Elementary school. This is such a helpful thing as your talents will bring some new drama and flair to the children and allow the teacher to have some much needed "extra" time for preparation, grading etc. 2 ways of spreading joy with one act!

August 22 – Spice Up Things with Your Own Herbs

Plant an herb garden. You'll love the ease in which you have these handy flavorful herbs with when they are right at your fingertips. You don't have to have a green thumb for this, just some time and a place to put them. Good Search (for Spreading Joy of course) and see for yourself.

August 23 – Clean Up as you Go

Pick up trash you see as you are walking on your route. We always try and do this. Normally there are trash cans at the entrance of any store, mall or fast food place. Just pick up what you see and drop it in the trash as you pass by. So easy, yet helpful!

August 24 – Help the Sick With Daily Items

Run Errands and or help clean around the house for a sick friend or someone that has just gotten out of the hospital. The gift of time is such a precious thing. Your time will allow them to rest, recuperate and to do so without feeling guilty that things are not getting done. This is such an easy, yet valuable way of spreading joy!

August 25 – Share Good News

Pass on positive news. Such a simple act of joy, but so overlooked. I think that ever single new station should have a 10 minute segment on something positive each time it airs. We can't change that, but we can email, tell, and announce on our websites the positive things going on in the world. Seek it out and be a part of spreading positive news.

August 26 – Reviews, Highlights and Articles

Do you own a blog or website? Do you have people reading what you write? Consider using your voice for Spreading Joy. Talk about the things we are doing throughout the year, like encouraging you to make a difference without spending a penny, helping you to find the joy in the ordinary and reminding you to do what you can where you are with what you have. During the times that we are having our Back to School event or Christmas Joy, write specific articles and then promote it on all of your social networking sites. Word of mouth is PRICELESS!

August 27 – Help at Church

Volunteer for your local church. Many people when they are hurting will turn to the church first. You will have many opportunities to make a difference for so many people that honestly need encouragement, hugs and inspiration.

August 28 – Hire a Teen

Pay a local Teenager to mow a neighbor's lawn. Two acts of spreading joy in one! The teenager will be happy for the extra funds and your neighbor will be thrilled that their lawn is taken care of for the week.

August 29 – Hey Mr. Mailman

Leave a note hanging in or on your mailbox thanking your mail carrier for always being so dependable! I confess, I should do this more often. I'm really thinking that once a month would be a nice way to say thank you as well as spreading joy his way.

August 30 – Design and Designate

Are you the artsy type that can whip up a design out of the air? Do you love playing around on the computer and creating amazing things such as logos, pictures etc? Sell these items and then donate a portion of your proceeds to Spreading Joy. Telling others that a portion of the proceeds will go to us will also be spreading the word about our efforts as well as helping you with yours. I love amazing partnerships.

August 31 – Animals Galore

Volunteer at an animal shelter. Help out with their paper work. Help keep the place clean. Play with the animals. Smile, laugh and enjoy all the hearty smooches from the animals there!

nuggetsofJOY:

➢ *Brighten someone's heart today – YOU matter. ~Marie Wikle*
➢ *It is possible to give without loving, but it is impossible to love without giving.--Richard Braunstein*
➢ *The best way to do good to ourselves is to do it to others; the right way to gather is to scatter.—Seneca*
➢ *A friend hears the song in my heart and sings it to me when my memory fails.—Anonymous*
➢ *What is a friend? A single soul dwelling in two bodies.—Aristotle*

September

While this book is full of positive reinforcement, inspiring ideas and ways to encourage, I also realize that sometimes we tire in well doing. We wonder if people see what we do, if they notice it or even care. Wondering about this can lead to thinking why bother, it doesn't matter anyway. May I encourage you to put that kind of thought out of your mind? It does matter. Spreading Joy and making a difference isn't about recognition, pat on the backs or high fives. It is about quietly reminding others through our actions that people care and everyone is able to make a difference if they simply choose to do so. Don't be weary in well doing. Every act of joy has a lasting effect.

September 1 – Did You Hear The One About...

Call someone who is not feeling well and talk until you make them laugh. You can truly brighten an otherwise dreary day for someone whose heart is heavy. This seems so simple, yet it is so valuable.

September 2 – Basket of Fruit

Leave a small basket of fruit for your mail carrier. They work hard; endure the weather and elements that nature throws at them and 99% of the time they have the warmest smile to give! Do something special for your mail carrier.

September 3 – Read and Pass On

Donate gently used magazines to a nursing home. Many people just toss out their magazines, but these can be used time and time again for the wonderful residents of many nursing facilities. Gather them up and drop them off today

September 4 – Let Me Help You

Ease someone's burdens today! A wonderful quote is "A friend doubles the joy and divides the pain." Divide the pain of someone today. The impact on their heart can literally be priceless as they feel like no one cares, no one will help and nothing matters anymore.

September 5 – My Gratitude List

Start a Gratitude Journal. Leave it out for others to see as they visit you. Listing all the wonderful little things that make your heart big will inspire others to take a look around and see what they have been missing.

September 6 – Soldiers Rule!

Encourage our soldiers. When you see military personnel, take the time to stop, look them in the eye, shake their hand and say thank you! They are giving their all to support our great Country and we can take the time to make a difference just by saying thank you. You'll be very surprised by how this touches them on such a deep level. When you take their hand to shake it, sneak in a hug!

September 7 – mmm mmm Good

Turn in your Campbell's Soup Labels. Do not think that this little act of joy is not helpful, as it truly is. Many schools use these to help purchase computers and items for their school. When you throw these away, you are throwing away money for schools

September 8 – Recycle & Reuse

Reuse your plastic bags at the grocery store or take them to the little recycle bin just outside the door. Are your bathroom trash cans small? Use the bag in those. Don't just throw them out. Recycle.

September 9 – Labor To Be Extra Kind

Labor Day is such an awesome way to end summer. Make it a point to be extra nice to anyone working! Go out of your way to be friendly to the store clerks and various people that you come in contact with today.

September 10 – Collection of Books

Organize a book drive. Get your neighborhood to donate gently used books. Pass out a flier asking for books – giving instructions to leave them in a bag on the porch letting them know you will pick them up the next week.

September 11 – Support our Military

Thank a Vet today! We Salute YOU! Purchase their dessert. Give them a hug. Look them in the eye and say thank you. Where would we be without their sacrifices and service? Where would our children be without their sacrifices? Thank them!

September 12 – Donate Plasma

Donate Plasma. And get paid for it. You are making a difference for others as well as helping your check book.

September 13 – Creativity Abounds

Share ideas on ways to make a difference. While I feel like I think about acts of joy differently than most, I would love to hear your ideas on how you have made a difference or how you think you can. Share! If I use your idea, I'll be sure to give you credit!

September 14 – Your Environment Loves You

Be nice to the environment; use a mug instead of adding to the trash today. Find a cute, adorable mug and use it daily!

September 15 – Books For The ER

Shop for books at yard sales and then leave them at a nearby Emergency Room. Many people drag their children with them to the emergency room, or their children are the cause of the visit. Either way, the books will come in handy to someone or you'll help the person that is hosting the yard sale!

September 16 – An Apple A Day

An Apple a day keeps the Dr. away, right? Well, have some fun with apples. Whip up your favorite apple based recipe with your family. Give a small basket of apples to a neighbor. Make the all time favorite candied apple

September 17 – You Can Smile

Smile at everyone you come in contact with today. Sounds so simple right? Have you actually tried it? You get on the elevator; everyone is quite, not speaking. Why not greet them with a huge smile and hearty hello? Don't wait for your cashier to greet you, greet him/her first with a warm smile. When you are walking down the hall, look people in the eye and smile. No matter what kind of horrible day you are experiencing, you'll feel better simply because you are smiling. Try it. Let me know how it changed your day.

September 18 – Thanks Vets!

Visit a VA hospital and drop off some cards for any of our Veterans! Take a moment and write a brief thank you note into 10 or 20 cards that you can get from the dollar store. Take them with you and give them away. Spend a moment with them, shake their hand and look into their eyes while saying thank you for serving our Country.

September 19 – Crafty In School

Donate unused craft items to a daycare or elementary school. I love scrapbooking, making cards and such. I try and use my scraps but tend to over purchase. If you are a scrap booker, you know what I'm talking about. Why not trim down your supplies and take some of those items you have been skipping over to your local elementary school or day care? Those kids will love it, their parents will benefit from their artwork and your heart will be flooded with great joy because you made a difference

September 20 – Fru-Fru Coffee is Awesome

Flavored Coffee Creamer for everyone! Can you imagine the surprise of your co-workers as they open the refrigerator and see an array of delicious creamers to dress up their morning coffee with? Put a note on the refrigerator door letting everyone know to check out the flavors and make sure you tell them to "please help yourself to the creamers" so they know it is for everyone.

September 21 – Thirsty for…..less

Do you open a new bottle of water every single day? If so, consider re-using the bottle by purchasing an inexpensive filtering system for your kitchen and a reusable water container. There are so many cute adorable water bottles out there as well as your everyday manly man containers too. I'm sure we can find one to suit your likes.

September 22 – Meal Time

Serve a meal at a homeless shelter or women's shelter. Want a perspective on your "not so great" home? Think your situation is not the greatest? An evening a month here will remind you that you are completely blessed as well as flood your heart with amazing joy as you smile, laugh and encourage these precious souls that are in these shelters. There is no telling how far this act of joy will carry the individuals that live here. Limitless possibilities!

September 23 – I Just Video'd To Say…

Make a video - If you know someone is having a rough day, make a video encouraging them to keep going and email it or facebook it to them. Just talk normally, as you would if they were sitting across from you. I have received a few of these, and LOVE it! They are normally unexpected and are sent at just the right time! I think I'll go and make one now!

September 24 – Free Babysitting

Babysit for a friend/neighbor for free. Many people are already scaling back their trips out, their dates with the love of their life simply because it can be expensive. Then you add the expense of a sitter on top of that – many just don't go. Why not offer one night a month to that wonderful Mom down the road, that single mom that is in your church or that couple that you love seeing hold hands all the time. You will love playing with the kids and then giving of yourself for free, you better get ready to open the flood gates of joy, because your heart will soar!

September 25 – Create Great Habits

Take the 30 Day Spreading Joy Challenge. We know it takes about 30 days to develop a habit and our desire is to have you spreading joy every single day. So we designed the 30 day challenge. Take 30 days and do 1 item a day for someone, anyone – related or random. Every week, email me and let me know how you are doing, if you've noticed your heart swimming in joy, if it's difficult or if you just need encouragement to make it through the entire 30 days! I will add your comments to our 30 Day Challenge Page so that it will encourage others to start their own journey of Spreading Joy!

September 26 – New Co-Worker = New Opportunities

Befriend a new co-worker. Starting in a new place is sometimes scary. You can't remember names and are learning the in's and out's of doing things. Not only befriend them but when you see another employee, call *that* employee by name, so the new co-worker has some help in remembering. Have a first day box waiting for them. Make sure it has a pen, pencil, stapler, pad, highlighter, paperclips, staples, a fun quote magnet and a few snacks from the vending machine. Imagine how your heart would have soared on your first day with a reception like this.

September 27 – And for the Person Behind Me

Order a McDonald's Hot Fudge Sundae for the vehicle behind you! Can you imagine the delight of their hearts? I know I would love this. Just do it. Don't worry about what they will think or what the person taking the order will think. Order it and smile big when you drive off.

September 28 – Celebrate Good Times

When your family goes out to eat to celebrate good times and there is cake involved, why not share with your server? If your family is anything like mine, we always have left over cake. We always leave some for those men and women who were our servers that evening, knowing they will get a break or even take it home. Sweet treats like this are very unexpected and the memory of your kindness will last a long time.

September 29 – Groovy Kind of Love

Give time to your spouse. When both husband and wife work outside the home, the quality time while at home becomes scarce. There are children to tend to, homework to check, never-ending clothes to wash. There is always something other than remembering why you fell in love in the first place. Do something together. Visit a park, book store or walk around the mall. Hold hands and talk, laugh and just enjoy the time you are spending together. Talk about the wonderful, million little things that make you happy.

September 30 – Thanks Officer

Thank a Police Officer today (hopefully NOT while you are getting a ticket!) You see them sitting in their cars doing reports. You pass them when you are having a meal. You are around many Officers and have an opportunity to encourage, inspire and motivate them simply with a warm smile, handshake and encouraging words such as "Thank you for protecting our community or I appreciate you." They put their lives on the line for us every day, the very least we can do is say thank you. Oh, should you happen to be getting a ticket – go ahead and say thank you anyway. It is their job and we did just break the law….right?

nuggetsofJOY:

- *Utilize those things you excel in and focus on taking one more step towards your dream today. ~ Marie Wikle*
- *Regarding our past: we can't change what happened, what we saw, what didn't happen or what we didn't see. We simply can learn from it and make changes to our future based on what we saw or didn't see. ~ Marie Wikle.*
- *Although the world is full of suffering, it is also full of the overcoming of it.--Helen Keller*
- *Courage is contagious. When a brave man takes a stand, the spines of others are stiffened.--Billy Graham*
- *Change is inevitable, growth is intentional.--Glenda Cloud*

October

I love this time of year. Days are shorter, nights are longer and joy fills the air with the anticipation of the holidays. People in general are happier, full of love and really start to focus on giving and making a difference. Take advantage of this! Encourage those around you to do more, talk about making a difference even more and be a light in someone's word.

October 1 – Absolutely No Negativity Today

Be Positive today. With the depressing economy, bills falling behind – this can really be tough, but it will encourage those around you and in the process bring joy to yourself. Truthfully speaking, no one likes being around Negative Nellie. Even when your whining is cute, like mine, it is still more encouraging to be positive!

October 2 – Penny Candy Days

Do you remember getting a small brown bag of candy over half full and only paying .25 cents for it? I do! I loved it and when I go places that have those kinds of candy; I always wish it was so much cheaper. Get bags of candy together and start a penny candy store. Invite the neighborhood kids and tell them to bring their pennies to shop with. Give a limit if necessary – of 25 items. Imagine the laughter and fun the kids will have shopping at your penny candy store/booth. If you do this, I would love for you to email me pictures so that we can showcase your store. I always help children at Christmas time and would love to have something like this for them. You can always send us boxes of candy. Order them in bulk online and ship directly to us. We have climate controlled storage for items such as this.

October 3 – Good Search for Spreading Joy

Instead of "googling" when searching, use Good Search at www.goodsearch.com and these guys will make a donation to Spreading Joy or other Non Profit. Good Search is powered by Yahoo so you know you are getting quality searches. They also will donate up to 30% of purchases from select stores online. This is a completely free way of donating to your favorite Non Profit or School simply by searching.

October 4 – I'm Forgiven

Forgive yourself today. Seriously! We carry around so much guilt for not doing things, for not being the kind of parent/person we want to be. Stop thinking those thoughts and move on. Give yourself permission to be completely human! You are going to make mistakes, you are going to fall short and as long as you get back up and move on, it's ok. Focus on the things that you do well and do them.

October 5 – A Treasure For a Lifetime

Crochet a baby blanket and give to a new Mom. She will love it! More than likely she will keep it and the child will have something from his/her childhood that is as old as they are. I love things like that. I personally have one monkey from my childhood that I received when I was 11. He is quite tattered and looks his age, but I wouldn't trade him for the world.

October 6 – Please!

Say Please and Thank you. You think that this would be something that we all do every day, but sadly enough it is not. We hurry through our day, not realizing that we are barking out demands, we neglect our manners when this truly can make someone's day. Imagine the huge impact a simple please or thank you has. So easy, yet often overlooked.

October 7 – Let Me Get That

When you are out to eat, pick up the tab of a perfect stranger. If you've never done this, do it. Call your server over to your table. Ask for the ticket of an individual and instruct them not to tell. Pay for it and send a note over on a napkin saying "Your bill has been paid in full as I'm spreading joy. Have a

JOYful evening." Then sit and watch or quietly slip out. Either way, you've done an awesome thing! You can also go to my website www.spreading-joy.org and print off the Spreading Joy Dinner Ticket. This is a beautifully done "ticket" that your waitress can give to the person that you've purchased their meal for.

October 8 – A Basket of Goodies For Waiting Family

Do you have a friend or family member in the hospital? Are people staying with them? Take biscuits to them on your way to work. When you have to eat out because you are staying with a loved one at the hospital, it gets expensive. Ease their burden and bring them great joy at the same time!

October 9 – Help Those that Help Others

Purchase items from those that give back. Look at my heroes section on my web site. I try to shop and/or use people that are there because they are doing what they can with what they have.

October 10 – You Can Do This

Share confidence. By uplifting and or motivating someone, they will remember that they "can do it!" This boost may come at just the right time for this person. Many simply overlook this opportunity to make a difference because they feel it is such a small insignificant thing, but think again. This is huge and the impact may be such that you may never know. Go ahead...share confidence with others.

October 11 – For You!

Give a gift card randomly. When you are at the register of any store, purchase a $20.00 gift card with your items. When the cashier hands you the gift card, write the amount on the little gift envelope and when you start to leave with your items, simply turn and hand the gift card to the person behind you. Their delight just might surprise you.

October 12 – Easy Kits for the Homeless

Purchase a pack of new socks for the homeless. Take ONE sock and put some travel size toiletries in them. Add in some candies, a few dollars and then stuff the match to the sock on top of all of that so that nothing falls out. Put several of these in your vehicle and when you come across someone in need, you'll have something very useful to give to them.

October 13 – Re-gifting Is Amazing

Do you own a company with items that are on clearance? Have you had a re-design on packaging? Donate those items to Spreading Joy and we'll use them as Christmas gifts or as prizes that we give away. There are limitless uses here. Gifts in kind go a very long way to help others.

October 14 – Mountain or Mole Hill

Leave the mole hill small. Avoid making this problem a mountain. You'll encounter enough mountains in your life time to stay focused on the small, annoying issues that tend to want to creep in and take over the day. Take a flower of life and plant in this tiny hill and make the best of a negative situation. Think about it in this fashion - what is it preparing you for?

October 15 – Never Enough Supplies for Kids

School has been in session for a little while now, but the supplies are still needed. Donate some pens, pencils and paper to a local school store. They sell and/or give these items to students who forget to bring in what they need.

October 16 – Walk for a Cure

Help someone fight cancer. Walk with them or for them on a cancer walk. Support them by helping with housework, errands or simple encouragement. Let them talk about anything they want or just BE THERE for them.

October 17 – Reese's Cup Fairy RULES

Be the Reese's Cup Fairy today! Reese's for EVERYONE! This is the greatest thing in the WORLD to do! Give freely! Give with a mile wide smile. Sneak one for yourself.

October 18 – Who Stole the Cookie…

Give Cookies in a jar! I love cookie jars but more than that, I love the cookies in them. You can bake cookies and put in them for a delicious gift, or purchase some delicious Oreo Golden Double Stuff and put in them. Have fun and get creative while giving this sweet treat!

October 19 – 10%....Really?

Support your local Church with an actual tithe offering. When is the last time you gave 10 % of your income to your church? I hope that you will consider this as many people will cut back their giving to the church first when things are tight.

October 20 – Here You Go, Sit Here

Give up your seat for someone. It doesn't matter if they are young or elderly. This type of kindness has long been forgotten and is HUGE in how it helps to bring about a positive change to those involved as well as those who see you make the offer.

October 21 – I'll Get That

Run errands for a new Mom. This is such a valuable gift of time. New Moms are zapped of energy and will appreciate the help. While you are there, do some small things like take out the trash and or clean the kitchen if necessary. Go one step further and ask if she'd like to nap while you watch the baby.

October 22 – Color Outside the Lines

Take coloring books and crayons by Children's ward at your local hospital. I know that many parents will thank you for your kindness. This will allow them to grab a few hours of time doing something fun without having to think about the current situation that has them in the hospital to begin with.

October 23 – Smore Please

Share S'mores! This microwavable dessert makes sharing laughter and smiles quick, easy and delicious! A half of graham cracker topped with a half of a chocolate bar and a marshmallow. Microwave for a 8-12 seconds and then top with the other half of the graham cracker. Laugh and smile as this ooey gooey dessert is consumed.

October 24 – Baby Needs You

Purchase some diapers, baby wipes and powders and donate to a local church nursery. This is especially handy if the church has an outreach to the underprivileged.

October 25

Buy some Halloween Candy and give it EARLY! Yes, early! Kids in your neighborhood would love to come home to a small baggie of candy that says Happy Halloween. It would take no time to package up some bags of candy and drop them off. Have fun and smile!

October 26 – Basket of Greatness

Take a basket of Trick o Treat candy to a shelter with children! Make it HUGE and put the greatest candies in it. Take it a few days before so that they will have something to look forward to. I've done this and the delight in the eyes of these children is indescribable.

October 27 – Sweet Surprise

Leave enough change in the vending machine for a snack or drink. Imagine the surprise of the person finding this. Such a little thing that will bring huge smiles.

October 28 – You Matter To Me

Let that certain someone in your life know just how important they are. Do not just assume they know, make sure they know. Tell them all the wonderful little things they he/she does that makes your heart smile.

October 29 – Everyone Loves Candy

Take Halloween Candy to a nursing home for the residents there. Yes, it's true that many cannot have sweets, but make up a bunch of bags filled with candy and a few with sugar free items and then everyone can enjoy the sweetness you are spreading all around.

October 30 – A little Extra Goes a Long Way

Leave an extra tip on your bill today! Regardless of what it was supposed to be, add in an extra $2.00. You will not miss it and your heart will thank you.

October 31 – Boo!

Give a cold drink to weary trick-o-treaters. I love taking my children out but would find that they would tire from the walking. One wonderful lady in our neighborhood was not only giving out delicious candy, but a cold 8 oz bottle of water to all the kids. Talk about genius! I was delighted as my children cooled off and was ready to continue gathering treats that night!

nuggetsofJOY:

- ➤ *Many look at failure as final, but it isn't. It's just a different road to get to where you need to go. ~ Marie Wikle*
- ➤ *Comparison is the thief of joy.—Unknown*
- ➤ *Seek not greatness, but seek truth and you will find both.--Horace Mann*
- ➤ *Be the one to step up, lend a hand and not expect anything in return. Do so with a smile! – Marie Wikle*
- ➤ *Let your thoughts meander towards a sea of ideas.--Leo D. Minnigh*

November

I hope that throughout the year you reflected on your blessings. While we tend to really narrow in on it during November, it's good to display our gratitude all year long. Start a new tradition this year by starting a weekly gratitude list. Take a piece of paper, put it on the refrigerator with everyone's name across the top and as each day passes, jot a few things down that you were thankful for. Put the date at the top and by this time next year, you'll have 52 pages reminding you of the great joy that filled your heart during the past year.

November 1 – Boo! again

Buy half price Halloween candy, pencils, bags and other fun items and take to homeless shelters. I always wonder if these children get to go trick-o-treating or not. Take the treats to them! Even splurge since things are half off!

November 2 – Gifts That Keep on Giving

Give a magazine subscription to someone. Buying them individually tends to get expensive. Purchase a magazine, make a reduced color photo of the front of the magazine, write on the back that a year's worth will be coming their way! Doing this for Christmas is a great present that will be enjoyed all year long. Doing this for NO reason is like extra sprinkles on your favorite cupcake!

November 3 – One Size Fits All

Give a HUG – my goodness, just do it! One size fits all, you can't hug the wrong person and even if you are having an awesome day, a hug will just make it fantabulous!

November 4 – Fav Raves

Find out what your childs "favorites" are. Jot them down and a few years later, ask again and see how it differs. You'll be surprised at the changes. I have several of these lists and it's always fun to listen to the delight in their voices and see the joy in their eyes when they are discussing why those shows are their favorites, those desserts are the greatest in the world and the songs that their hearts love to sing.

November 5 – It Never Hurts To Ask

Ask your employer if your organization can collect toys for Spreading Joy's Christmas JOY event. If you are outside of the Charlotte Metro area, maybe you could support us with a Gift Card Drive. Collect gift cards in the amount of $10.00 and then mail them to us. McDonald's and Wal-Mart Gift cards work well for everyone.

November 6 - Vote

VOTE – Don't let this opportunity pass you by. So many men and women gave their life and even stood alone for this right. Let your voice be heard!

November 7 – Be Part of the Solution

Help solve a problem, do not just give advice on how to do it. We are all busy and it seems that every where we turn people are always giving us advice on how to do things better, more efficient and/or how to fix things. Instead of just giving the advice, why not offer to help with it? Take that advice to the next level and make a huge difference. What I wouldn't give for some spreading joy heroes that did this!

November 8 – Be Bold

Fearlessly BE yourself! I saw this quote a long time ago and fell in love with it. We need YOU to simply be authentically you. You are made to be amazing, don't try and be someone you are not. Grow your strengths, focus on your abilities and make the best of each day!

November 9 – Fun Time Waiting

Take M&M's to Local Hair Salon and leave for patrons. Many bring in their children and this will be a pleasant surprise. Many adults will giggle like kids when they realize these sweet, colorful candies are free for the taking. Put a card on the basket that says "I'm spreading joy your way... for ideas on how YOU can make a difference please visit www.spreading-joy.org" and you'll be spreading joy more than one way.

November 10 – Nothing Like Efficiency

Replace all of your lightbulbs with energy efficient ones! This will help our environment as well as save you some cold hard cash.

November 11 – Coupons Last Longer With our Troops

Donate expired manufacturers coupons to the troops overseas. I hate throwing money away, so giving coupons here helps to stretch the value of these coupons even more. http://www.grocerysavingtips.com/expiredgrocerycoupons.htm has a listing of where we can send those coupons that are good for an additional 6 months. The list is always changing, so make sure you check often!

November 12 – Joyfully Made

Do you make your own jewelry? Make a few pieces that have JOY on it and donate to us. We will use these items as a means of spreading joy and list you on our Heroes page, along with a link back to your site

November 13 – Men...You Rock

Make cards for all the wonderful guys in your life. Putting a personal note in the card to let this great guy know just how special he truly is. Encourage him by saying how proud HIS father would be or if he is YOUR son, tell him how proud you are.

November 14 – We Want Your Ideas

Email me with YOUR ideas of Spreading Joy that are not in this book and I'll include them along with credit back to you in my next book or on my site. Who knows, you may even see YOUR idea in a Spreading Joy App.

November 15 – Engage and Encourage

ENGAGE with US over at facebook! Simple but encouraging. You aren't limited to 140 characters and some of the interactions and ideas are simply amazing.

November 16 – Sunshine On My Shoulder Makes Me Happy

Purchase sun catcher art sets and distribute to neighborhood kids. This is particularly fun in the summer time. The days are lazy and long and the children are looking for something different to do. If you want to create lasting memories for them, bring along something to drink and work on a sun catcher for yourself. The laughter will cause your smile to shine for days.

November 17 – A Little Goes a LONG Way

Send a little extra gift to your favorite Non Profit Organization! As a Non Profit that can only give when others give, I understand how important $5.00 here and $10.00 there is. Never, ever discount what you may consider as a "little". You may never know when that little bit helped someone take the next step to greatness.

November 18 – Go Green

Green is GORGEOUS! Use all plastic containers for lunch today! No adding to the trash! Talk about easy? This is a wonderful way to make a difference, save some green while reminding yourself and others that green is gorgeous!

November 19 – Schooch on In

Snuggle! Just enjoy some time sitting close with your mate. Read, watch TV or simply listen to his/her heartbeat.

November 20 – Childhood Delight

Yahoo!! Give out these delicious drinks today! This chocolaty drink was a staple in our home when our children were little. It brought so many smiles and still does. The kids remember the fun days of summer and the bottle with the bright yellow label on it.

November 21 – Leftovers are Awesome

Mail your unused Gift Cards to Spreading Joy! This cost you nothing and will be so very valuable to us!

November 22 - Sacrifice

Give sacrificially today. This is not the easiest thing as it requires faith, but it is so rewarding. Giving 10 or 15% towards your favorite charity will enable them to do a little more than normal and encourage the organization more than you could possibly know. Give till it hurts. Are you willing to do without to make a difference?

November 23 – Time to Catch Up

Seek out an old friend and just catch up. Be it over the phone, Facebook chat, email or in person, you'll both be glad you did. Time is short, things will always need to be done and someone will always want your attention but these few hours or even moments will last a life time on your heart.

November 24 – Don't Wish… Be!

BE the change you want to see in the world! There are so many things we think should be fixed, changed or made better. Start with YOU! Whatever you are thinking on a broad scale, bring it home and start with yourself. Be the nicer person you wish to see, give a little more than others expect, hold your head a little higher and smile more. Do not just wish for change, be the change.

November 25 – Thankfulness…Always

Give a Thanksgiving Dinner to a needy family! Make their day by providing the turkey, dressing, veggies and yumilicious dessert! Your heart will be flooded with amazing joy when you make this delivery.

November 26 – A Simple Thank You

Say Thank you. Be Thankful. Express your gratitude. JOY is contagious, so when you are noticing the wonderful little things that make your heart soar, others will notice things around them, and then others will notice and so on, and so on…. You get the picture. Be aware of the things that make you smile and say thank you. Point them out by telling someone what a great thing that was, or huge deal that is. You'll help many others to be aware of the joy that surrounds them just by being thankful.

November 27 – Help for Newlyweds

Know a couple that just got married this year? Give them a bag of Christmas decorations. It's exciting to set up your first Christmas tree and decorate your home for the first time, but it can be very expensive. Try and find out what they like or go with the generic angels, stars, candy canes and gingerbread men. You'll help make their first Christmas together a memorable one.

November 28 – mmmmm Chocolate

When the holidays are approaching, carry some inexpensive candy around with you and give freely. Give Kisses at Valentine's Day, bells at Christmas time, etc. You will definitely sweeten up someone's day when you are spreading joy this way!

November 29 – Toy, Toys, Toys

Make a Financial Contribution to Spreading Joy for TOYS! We are always looking for toys! You can do this in July, February or even December when it's needed most. We always want to give more and make a bigger difference than before. Will you help here?

November 30 – Trimming the Tree

Hold a Christmas Tree trimming party and ask guest to bring one pantry item and one toiletry item for a local Battered Women's Shelter. You'll have help with decorating your tree and allow others to give and make a difference, not to mention the laughter, food and fun!

nuggetsofJOY:

> ➤ *What awaits you is as vast as the ocean. Embrace the day, seize the precious moments and treasure the beauty of it all. ~ Marie Wikle*
> ➤ *Never discount the power of a smile, a hug or the simple words, "I love you". Completely POWERFUL ~ Marie Wikle*
> ➤ *Joy is very infectious; therefore, be always full of joy.-- Mother Teresa*
> ➤ *Make one person happy each day and in forty years you will have made 14,600 human beings happy for a little time at least.--Charley Willey*
> ➤ *Too many people today know the price of everything and the value of nothing.--Ann Landers*
> ➤ *I'm thankful this...right here, right now ~ Marie Wikle*

December

Merry Christmas everyone! As you are busy with family, parties, purchasing and wrapping gifts don't forget to slow down and enjoy the little things that make life big. Instead of a mad dash through the mall, go and enjoy the decorations, the smells and music. Enjoy your family and the various gatherings you'll have. If things aren't perfect, don't sweat it, simply enjoy being together.

December 1 – Christmas is Almost Here

Start collecting toys and/or gift cards for Spreading Joy! WE need YOUR help! With the desire to make a difference for so many children we realize we can not do it without your help.

December 2 – Stop the Joy Thieves

BE nice as you are shopping. At Christmas time many people are in such a hurry and lose their cool easily. If this happens to you, just smile and be nice. Realize that tensions are high and tempers will flair and don't be apart of spreading ick!

December 3 – Stocking Were Hung

Buy very "cool" Christmas Stockings for your kids! Don't just get the red ones with the white fluff at the top. Find them something that they will love and can cherish for years to come. Their likes, loves and favorites change, so use that and surprise them with a wonderful new stocking this year!

December 4 – Tick Tock

Time is ticking by ever so quickly! Keep spreading joy daily! Look for the opportunities around you to make a difference. Take some time to visit our website and tell us your story of how you are making a difference. Everyone has a story to tell. You never know who you'll inspire when you share your ideas. Tell us, motivate us and inspire us!

December 5 – What Makes Your Day?

Take pictures of things that make your day. Post them on flicker, Facebook etc. for all to see. You may remind someone of some very simple, yet special treasures.

December 6 – Christmas JOY

Talk to your Company/Church about collecting toys for Christmas Joy. This is easy and a wonderful gift of giving especially if you are anywhere near Charlotte/Metro area of NC. If you are not near us, and would love to help out, consider doing a gift card collection. Collect $10.00 gift cards to McDonalds, Wal-Mart, Target etc. This will help out so much as many of these cards are used just in case we run out of age appropriate gifts. Email me for a flier and other ideas to get your group excited about giving the GIFT of giving!

December 7 – Opportunities To Encourage

Make it a point to encourage today -You'll NEVER know how you affect someone! It could be your words of encouragement today that help someone to move past that mental road block or their dark cloud that has been lingering over them to vanish entirely today. Look for genuine opportunities to encourage someone today!

December 8 – Chili Cook off

Have everyone bring in a crock pot full of their favorite chili and vote on who has the best. Charge $3.00 per person, get some of the 2 oz cups and give everyone some of each kind. Donate the funds you collect to your favorite charity. You'll have tons of fun and eat really well that day. Make the grand prize a couple of hours off with pay or a gift certificate that was donated for the event.

December 9 – Kids Art Touch Heart

Get your kids to write notes/draw pictures for others. I love to receive cards and pictures from kids. They are so very honest and adorable. You never know what to expect and that is ok because these kinds of gifts are from their precious little hearts and mean so much. Encourage your kids to do this while you are making dinner. Double JOY is always wonderful as you'll have time to prepare and they will be touching hearts!

December 10 – Quotable Stickies

Write your favorite quotes on post it notes and leave in various places. Many people may have never even seen that particular quote. You may inspire someone to read more quotes which will brighten their day. Go, shine brightly!

December 11 – Locks of Love

Donate your gorgeous hair to the Locks of Love program. They are giving beauty to those who feel anything but beautiful.

December 12 – Adopt A Family

Christmas is right around the corner and many are in need. Get together with your children and adopt a family. With a little research your family can be a huge inspiration to another family. Get them everything they'd need for a scrumptious meal as well as toys for their children. You choose gifts for the parents and then, allow your children to pick something that they want to give the kids. Allow them to wrap and write out the tag and watch in amazement as your children's heart soars because they are making such a huge difference.

December 13 – Small Baskets Produce Huge Hearts of Gratitude

Make a few small fruit baskets and deliver to a local hospital/nursing home. This is a very inexpensive way to brighten someone's day. Get a basket from the dollar store, a few apples, orange, some grapes, banana and a few candies make it simply delicious. Add a cute bow and card that expresses how you care if it is for someone you know. Take this idea to the next level by getting 7 people together and each one of you get something different. Have coffee/tea, play some music and enjoy the laughter while assembling your baskets.

December 14 – Gift Baskets

Give a basket of goodies to someone today. Find out what their favorite things are and make it a fun survival kit wrapped up and sealed with a bow on top. What coffee lover wouldn't love a basket of various coffees, a mug, various creamers and chocolate dipped spoons? Movie lovers would love a basket of popcorn, snacks and a few dvd's to keep and use when the mood strikes them. Baskets make it easy to give in style!

December 15 – It's A Date

Make sure you schedule time to play. Sounds so simple doesn't it? This time of year we are so busy doing for others, making lists and checking it twice that we forget about spreading joy to ourselves. This may sound selfish, but if you do something simple yet satisfying for yourself, then you'll have a much easier time making a difference for someone else. Besides, we normally don't play alone do we? Have fun, play hard and enjoy the huge smiles!

December 16 – Party for Others

Host a Christmas Party, ask guests to bring a toy for underprivileged kids. You'll enjoy the gift of giving an opportunity for your guests to make a difference. As everyone arrives, have them put the gifts under your beautifully decorated tree.

December 17 – Light Up their Hearts

Prepare a candlelight dinner for your family. This can done very elegantly without a lot of effort and cost. Put out your best dishes, use wedges of lettuce for a fancy salad. Purchase a bag of shrimp for shrimp cocktail and place around the edges of fancy glasses that you've purchased from the dollar store. A rotisserie chicken you've purchased or made yourself along with some bread and veggies are a pure delight. Don't forget dessert! Cheese cake dressed up with fruit or chocolate is simple, yet amazing. Arrange several candles on the table, nice table cloth and you've got an amazing evening planned for your family without a lot of effort!

December 18 – Passion Is a Great Thing

Be completely passionate about all that you do today. Find 3 or 4 things to focus on and passionately pursue them. Your determination and passion will spark a longing in others to do the same. Think about it… passionately Spreading Joy! Talk about contagious; you'll be infecting everyone's attitude with great desires for joy today.

December 19 – Looking Good

Give free haircuts to those in need. Find a local homeless shelter or women's shelter and volunteer once a month to simply trim hair. Get with the administrator and iron out what you can and can't do. If you don't cut hair yourself, find several others that specialize in this and make a huge difference for a lot of people.

December 20 – Party For Others

Get a group of friends together, make up some bags of fruit, snacks and candies and take to a local nursing home. Wear your Santa hats and sing Christmas Carols for them. Plan ahead and find out when a good time would be so that everyone can be gathered in their common area. Many will sing with you, smile and even cry tears of joy because you cared enough to bring Christmas to them.

December 21 – Awesome Lunch

Make 20 sack lunches and pass out to homeless in your area. A loaf of bread, meats, cheeses, pack of chips and a Reese's Cup for dessert will be such a wonderful meal for the homeless in your area. Don't forget something to drink with the lunch. When you read this, it seems so very small but trust me, this is extremely huge!

December 22 – These Ladies Are Special

Take a box full of toiletries items to Women's shelter. Include the personal items that many ladies need each month as well as some lotions and such to pamper themselves with. No matter where you live, ladies need to be able to pamper themselves from time to time.

December 23 – The Non Starving Artist

Display your child's art on Flickr or Facebook. Why stop at the fridge? Show off your child's handy work for the entire world to see!

December 24 – Merry Christmas Eve

It's Christmas Eve. Many people are running around like mad doing a million last minute things. Stop and purchase some hot chocolate or various drinks and share! This simple act will remind people of the reason for the season and maybe…just maybe, remove some frustrations while flooding them with joy. Just park yourself outside a local store (with permission of course) and spread some joy.

December 25 – Merry Christmas

DWELL on the Blessings of the Year! Don't just think of a few for a few moments. Really take some time to dwell on them. Search your heart for all the good that you've seen, experienced and had the pleasure of having this year. If you are a blogger, blog it and then make sure you @ me on it on twitter or the Spreading Joy Fan page on Face Book. I would be honored to check it out as well as share it with others.

December 26 – Christmas Joy and Sales are Made for Each Other

Donate Christmas Wrapping Paper to Spreading Joy. Don't you love when wrapping paper goes on sale? I surely do. I try and stock up each year because I know my heart wants to give so many presents to children the next year. Go and enjoy those after Christmas sales but don't forget Spreading Joy!

December 27 - *Waving*

Wave at everyone you see! I can NOT tell you just how much fun this is. I am usually walking somewhere and will do this. I like to see how many waved back verses how many didn't. And, if you can get someone to honk at you, well now, that is just icing on the cake.

December 28 – I'm Sorry

Don't play the blame game today. Step up and own your mistakes. You'll surprise those around you and set a standard for the day. It's so easy to place blame and take the high road without looking back. Spreading joy is not always easy, but always beneficial. Step up and lead the way on this act of joy.

December 29 – Another Year Awaits YOU

Can you believe this year is almost over? Start thinking of ideas for Spreading Joy next year. Plan on how you can be one of the many that will be spreading joy daily! Plan on sharing, inspiring and motivating others to making a difference. Don't think of it as resolutions, think of it as a way of life.

December 30 – Don't Let the Kids Have all the Fun

Play in the snow with your kids. If you live in a region where it snows often, enjoy being a KID again. Bundle up and plan on laughing and having a glorious time. Throw snowballs, make snow angels and build the snowman that is destined to take over the world! The housework, reports for the day job and all other grown up stuff can wait! Go, play and make some lasting memories before your children grow up and move out.

December 31 – Pass That Book My Way

Enjoy reading? Pass along some of your books! Pass along **this** book to someone and spread some JOY their way. Why not jot a note in it saying "I'm spreading joy your way! Enjoy this book and then pass along to others!" date it and add your name. It would be really cool for someone to get the book, come to the "how are you spreading joy" page and say that they received it in this fashion. Pretty awesome if you ask me!

nuggetsofJOY:

- *Hug the ones you can, call the ones you can't and the one you can't call....honor their memory today in a special way. ~ Marie Wikle*
- *Most folks are about as happy as they make up their minds to be.--Abraham Lincoln*
- *Be as upbeat as you can be. The basic success orientation is having an optimistic attitude.--John DePasquale*
- *Motivation is what gets you started. Habit is what keeps you going.--Jim Ryun*
- *He conquers who endures. —Persius*
- *When you are surrounded by hurt, use that to deepen your drive to make a difference! Sacrifice more, give more and resolve to do what you can.~ Marie Wikle*

A HUG is......

LOVE wrapped around you so tight

WARMTH when your heart feels cold

PEACE when the ocean within you rages

A SMILE when the tears flow

COURAGE when fear abounds

FULLNESS when the soul feels empty

DELICIOUS when the world tastes bitter

HARMONIOUS when your life is out of tune

HEALING for the one that is grieving

KINDNESS in the midst of hatred

STRENGTH for those weakened by the journey

WISDOM when confusion is all around

ENCOURAGEMENT when you feel defeated

PURE JOY when happiness is hiding

A WELCOME HOME after the day has been cruel

REASSURANCE when all confidence is lost

CERTAINTY when all is unsure

PRICELESS when the heart feels worthless

EXTRAORDINARY when typical over throws the day

MYSTERIOUS as the miracle of its uniqueness takes form

A WHISPER – *I love you*

HUGS – Do you cherish these priceless miracles?

Thank You...

for delighting in my delight
for noticing when I need to be noticed
for paying attention to what makes me happy
and knowing no gesture is too small
for loving me as always
and the humor that makes me giggle - sometimes 3 days later
for the hugs everyday, so little to most but so HUGE in my
eyes
for calling when you can
for helping me get through the day
for always knowing...always!
for honestly communicating with me
and allowing me to see you through
for the sparkle in my eye when I see your eyes sparkle
for the words that inspire me to give more
for listening when I need to empty my heart and soul of hurt
for guidance when I feel lost
thank you for all the treasures that you give to my heart
for the smile that lights my face each day
for the unexpected kindness you flood me with
for accepting me just as I am
and encouraging the little girl in me to run free
for your amazing smile that chases away gloom.......

Thank You

Think you're too small to make a difference? Think again!

- Put a tiny rock in your shoe and walk a mile
- Give a simple sucker to a toddler & watch their world light up
- Try ignoring that fly buzzing about your meal
- Leave that piece of dust under your contact
- Smile widely with a tiny piece of black pepper stuck to your tooth
- Watch what the ants will do with your slice of pie
- Remember the grain of sand that became a gorgeous pearl
- Think about the one smooth stone that took out a giant
- Notice how one spark can consume an entire forest
- One flicker of light pierces the darkest night
- 1 person "going" for it, gives courage to the fearful
- A reassuring smile brings hope
- Gaze at the GIANT oak that was once a tiny seed
- One single tear can soften the hardest heart
- The difference of one second.... That allowed you to miss that accident or plane crash
- Ignore that nail in your tire
- Leave that splinter in your finger

I Wish

I wish I knew what was going on
I wish you'd let me see
I wish I could bring you smiles
Just the way that you do me

I wish I could melt the hurt away
I wish you'd let me in
I wish for you great happiness
And that your heart will soar high again

I wish away the sorrow
I wish away the dread
I wish you a thousand blessings
Upon your life instead

I wish you every kindness
I wish you joy and peace
I wish you amazing laughter
And great love that's within reach

I wish these great things for you
And even a million more
And for every one that's granted you
I wish for hope restored.

I Resolve to....

We all waltz into the New Year thinking of things we want to accomplish during the year.

I hope that my list of resolutions will inspire you to boldly resolve to make resolutions that truly matter.

Doing this will inspire you as well as those around you.

I resolve to make the best of whatever comes my way each day

I resolve to smile daily, even if it's through tears

I resolve to encourage my family to be their best, even when the worst is flooding our world

I resolve to enjoy the success of others and encourage them to keep pursuing their passion

I resolve to treat others the way I want to be treated, no wait... BETTER than I want to be treated

I resolve to be kind to those who are the meanest

I resolve to listen to my heart and not feel guilty for doing things for myself

I resolve to do what I can with what I have and enJOY it

I resolve to read a book a month (or listen...as I love audio books)

I resolve to be a positive force

I resolve to use my strengths without worry about how my weaknesses may come across

I resolve to allow my heart to sing freely

I resolve to find beauty in the Ordinary

I resolve to laugh daily....regardless (hey, if I'm gonna cry often, I may as well laugh even more)

I resolve to hug freely

I resolve to say thank you to someone daily

I resolve to learn from my mistakes

I resolve to face difficulties with courage

I resolve to let those in my world know just how important they truly are

I resolve to continue to be Matthew 5:16

I resolve to be compassionate

I resolve to let the hurt & disappointment that surrounds me to make me more determined

I resolve to keep taking the next step, even when I can't see the path

I resolve to love, and do so freely

I resolve to celebrate the good, forgive the bad and enjoy the moment

I resolve to change what I can, fix what is wrong & find the good in the rest

I resolve to reflect on the blessings of the day at the end of the day

I resolve to celebrate small victories and push onward through challenges

I resolve to be content with what I have, while striving to improve where I can

I resolve to not allow circumstances to dictate HOW I live

I resolve to not allow guilt to eat at my heart

I resolve to stop and smell the roses when I'm near them

I resolve to believe that I'm enough and not compare myself to others

Resolve to do what you can, where you are with what you have…..without feeling guilty!

Thank You!

Thank you for how you are Spreading Joy and making a difference. Thank you for your heart for others. Thank you for reminding people, by your actions, that everyone can make a difference.

Don't ever forget that every single act of joy you do for someone else has limitless possibilities.

You matter! You truly do!

Have fun Spreading Joy!

For more ideas and encouragement, please visit us at www.spreading-joy.org

You can also LIKE our page at www.facebook.com/spreadingjoycorp

Hugs Yall

Marie